# The
# Alphabet
# in My Hands

# Marjorie Agosín

# The Alphabet in My Hands

## A Writing Life

Translated by Nancy Abraham Hall

RUTGERS UNIVERSITY PRESS

New Brunswick, New Jersey, and London

Library of Congress Cataloging-in-Publication Data

Agosín, Marjorie.

    The alphabet in my hands : a writing life / Marjorie Agosín ;
translated by Nancy Abraham Hall.

      p.   cm.

    ISBN 0-8135-2704-X (cloth : alk. paper)

    1. Agosín, Marjorie.   2. Authors, Chilean–20th century Biography.

1. Title.

PQ8098.1.G6Z466   1999

861–dc21

  [B]                                               99-23069

                                                  CIP

British Cataloging-in-Publication data for this book is available from the British
Library

Manufactured in the United States of America

To my children, Joseph and Sonia,
who taught me the beauty of
invisible things and gave me
a new alphabet to love

# contents

## part 1: childhood

## Part 2: Journey to the Other America

# Acknowledgments

Generous spirits accompanied me as I journeyed in the uncertain realm of memory and the passions of the imagination. I am grateful for the presence of my parents, my husband, dear friend Alida Brill, Steven Schouer, Paul Roth, and Monica Bruno.

I want to especially thank Leslie Mitchner, editor at Rutgers University Press, for her presence. Her vision, inspiration, and commitment to the writing life has made the *Alphabet* truly possible. I also want to thank Brigitte Goldstein for her loving eye and her clarity of vision and language. My deep gratitude goes to Nancy Hall, colleague and friend, for her admirable translation.

I also want to acknowledge the presence of an invisible reader somewhere who on his or her way to work or in the quiet delicacy of a summer afternoon will join me in the reading of the *Alphabet* and will be a witness to a shared memory.

# Introduction

Poised on the western edge of South America, long and narrow Chile has been the site of several political experiments since 1970: democratic socialism, military dictatorship, and, most recently, free-market economics. The transition to this latest phase was, on the surface, a peaceful one, leading some observers to assume that Chile was reconciled to the past, committed to repairing treacherous fault lines within its social fabric. This illusion was recently shattered by the detention in London of ex-dictator Augusto Pinochet, charged by Spain with genocide and crimes against humanity. While Spanish and British magistrates worked to establish legal precedent in this groundbreaking case, the world was once again reminded of the horrors perpetrated by the state following the bloody overthrow of President Salvador Allende in September of 1973. During the seventeen years Pinochet ruled Chile, more than three thousand people were killed or "disappeared," and tens of thousands more were imprisoned or forced into exile.

Tragically, almost no one has been punished for the junta's excesses. Chile's democratic government, reestablished in 1988, has been anxious to appease powerful businessmen and members of the armed forces who consider Pinochet a national hero. Like most of the nation's citizens, the current Chilean government has chosen to forget and move on. One of the most unique and eloquent voices raised against continued silence and in favor of memory is that of poet Marjorie Agosín, a native of Chile, and award-winning promoter of international understanding and human rights. *The Alphabet in My Hands* is the story of her life that was deeply affected by Pinochet's bloody crusade to save Chile from communism.

In two earlier volumes, *A Cross and a Star* and *Always from Somewhere Else*, Marjorie Agosín recalled what it was like for her Jewish parents to grow up in predominantly Catholic Chile. Both her mother's story and her father's evoke the joys and struggles of those raised in the confluence of two cultures at odds with one another at midcentury. Like her parents, Marjorie Agosín lived those contradictions, and more. In *The Alphabet in My Hands*, she writes about her own privileged childhood in Chile, her family's sudden flight into exile during Allende's tenure, a lonely adolescence in southern Georgia, and finally, personal and professional maturity in New England, where she has been a distinguished member of the Wellesley College faculty since 1982.

The first half of *The Alphabet in My Hands*, devoted to the poet's childhood and early adolescence, opens with "Calendar," a series of lyrical evocations of the special occasions that marked the rhythm of the young writer's first fourteen years. Raised with loving awareness of her Jewish roots, she nevertheless participates in many Catholic rituals and celebrations through the agency of her nanas who secretly baptized her in the hopes of saving her soul. As she looks back on her family's celebrations of Passover, Rosh Hashanah, and Yom Kippur, she also remembers thrilling forays into the nighttime garden on St. John's Eve and community processions at the water's edge in honor of St. Peter. While her family maintains an open-minded attitude toward the dominant culture—an aunt organized Easter egg hunts, her mother admired the beauty of the golden altars found in Catholic churches—the writer is nevertheless keenly aware of her dual identity. At once a participant and an outsider, she is always on the margins with regard to her country and its Catholicism. As she recalls how she searched for colored eggs buried in the moist April earth of the south Pacific coast, her thoughts turn to those members of her extended family who had to hide to avoid persecution in Europe: "Perhaps that was what it meant to be Jewish, to suffer the wind of God on the back of our necks while we prayed, and to feel our hands buried in the soil, while we looked for rabbits steeped in the wisdom of the earth, celebrating an act of faith as communion, dressed in dreams."

A dreamlike quality also characterizes the author's recollections of happy summers spent with her family in Quisco, a small beach community not far from Santiago. Fresh baked bread, long walks along rocky paths, and an unhurried pace at the beach contributed each summer to the young writer's developing sensibilities: "It was probably in that small stone house by the sea that I first glimpsed the shudder and the sound of poetry, communion with the living and the dead." The family's stays at the shore also afforded Marjorie Agosín a deeper knowledge of her own body, and a reprieve from the socioeconomic divisions that characterized the society at large. The writer recalls the delight of donning white slacks and heading for Quisco's tiny movie theater after dark, where intellectuals and fishermen sat side by side on folding chairs, talking freely to the projectionist about their favorite scenes. "There were no distinctions between rich and poor, summer residents and natives. In certain ways, the movies . . . made us feel equal, like a family, accomplices in that world of illusion up on the screen."

The chasm that separates the privileged from those less fortunate in any society laid an early claim to Marjorie Agosín's attention. As a child she stands on her grandmother's balcony in Valparaiso and wonders about the people who live in the small dwellings dotting the hills of the city, fragile houses at the mercy of the elements: "The rain was angry, sweeping away the humble tables, the fragile roofs of tin and cardboard" while in "the other Chile" it danced on oversized windows, and children like herself "ate toast and hot chocolate." Against her grandmother's wishes she befriends Magda, the woman who begs at the corner. She corresponds with a leper relegated to the far ends of the Pacific, and spends time with Soledad, a mentally retarded girl. She watches the many refugee women who, thanks to her mother's generosity, pass through her house on their way to resettlement in Chile. Clearly the interest in and compassion for women and children from all walks of life, a hallmark of Marjorie Agosín's adult writing, took root in the young poet's early years.

Yet the kindness that she regularly extended to others and the peaceful inclusion she experienced each summer in Quisco were not to be found at the tiny, prestigious British school she and her sister attended in Santiago. In "Being Jewish" Marjorie Agosín records painful memories of that school, where the songs and snubs of students and teachers made a small Jewish girl feel extremely unwel-

come. As she explores this early trauma, she also celebrates its fe-
licitous consequence: the Agosín children were transferred to Santiago's Hebrew Institute, where they flourished.

While the institute afforded the young writer a secure and happy
space in which to learn, she continued to grow in awareness of people and practices that excluded or demeaned her as a Jew in Chile.
From the central role of godmothers in the lives of her Catholic
neighbors, to offensive figures of speech used by upper-class dinner
companions oblivious to her heritage, painful memories are summoned as she recalls her formative years. Certainly the Holocaust
stories she heard from her mother and grandmothers as well as the
family photograph albums, filled with pictures of radiant young aunts
she would never meet, contributed to her understanding of her family's history and the unspeakable horrors they had been made to en-
dure because they were Jewish.

Indeed, many years before her own family found it necessary to
move to the United States, Marjorie Agosín was aware of the chal-
lenges of exile, the courage required to start over in a strange land,
and the inevitable sense of loss such a move entailed. In "The
Women," she draws loving portraits of her grandmothers and great-
grandmothers, travelers and survivors who crossed borders and
oceans in search of a new home. A tiny sky-blue suitcase filled with
antique jewels and pendants evokes precious memories of Helena,
who was partial to white doves and sugar, yet never recovered her
true self once forced to leave Vienna; Sonia, whose deep, soothing
voice intoned lullabies in Yiddish; Raquel from Odessa, who collected unusual shoes; and Hanna, renamed Josefina by a customs in-
spector and known as Chepi to her family, the least traumatized of
her immigrant forebears, a knitter of scarves who could not boil water but loved Chile deeply from the moment she arrived on the back
of a mule.

In addition to her grandmothers, the poet pays homage to the
women who nurtured her in Santiago. These aptly named
"Guardians of Childhood" are her beloved nanas whose stained
aprons, earthy fragrances, murmured prayers, and loving gestures
are forever etched into the writer's consciousness. The wisdom of the
nanas' legends, the pain and allure of their poverty, and the stead-
fastness of their loyalty constituted important lessons for the child

who relished mornings in the kitchen, late afternoons gossiping at the curb in a rickety straw chair, and evenings in the back rooms, where the aroma of boldo tea and the melodrama of radio soap operas filled the air. In her adult dreams Marjorie Agosín summons one nana in particular, her beloved Carmencha, recalling her soft steps, her deep gaze, and above all, her tenderness as she put the children to bed: "As always, she promised me love. She kissed my eyelids. She returned time and again to the plains of my ears, singing in the language of her ancestors, of fire and ashes her hands of sulphur and maize." From the nanas the poet learned the simple pleasure of being alive, the strength to withstand prejudice and renounce permanence, and above all, the ability to comfort and protect others from the sidelines, the rooms at the back of the house.

The second half of *The Alphabet in My Hands* is devoted to the writer's life in exile, and begins with "Time of Ire," a recapitulation the traumatic events of 1973: first, a journey to war-torn Israel, and later the bloody coup in Chile which resulted in the death of Salvador Allende, her grandmother's childhood beau and president of Chile. The tense scenarios of war in the Middle East and political turmoil at home are recalled briefly, tersely, as if there were few words with which to describe the historical moments that permanently marked the sensitive girl of fourteen. The writer quickly moves on to recount her family's flight from the only home she had ever known to exile in the United States, where her father had secured a teaching job as a professor of chemistry.

The sudden and abiding loss of all that was familiar—home, garden, grandparents, nanas, teachers, classmates, clothing, furniture, and above all, her beloved Spanish language—is detailed in "Pilgrimages," a heartbreaking chapter about Marjorie Agosín's struggle for connection and acceptance at Clark Central High School in Athens, Georgia. Ostracized and mocked as an immigrant with a strange accent, the writer's high school years are made worse by the bone-chilling news from Chile—prisoners, missing people, three classmates disappeared, one shot—and the anguish of seeing her beautiful mother forlorn and lonely. While the fragrant magnolias offered a modicum of comfort and beauty to them both, the pain of exile and loss was excruciating: "I came home each day to console my mother, weeping over the piles of letters she had thrown on the floor. The kitchen pots were always empty. There were no fragrant rubber plants, no kites, and my father became ever more fragile and silent."

Just as her nana Carmencha used to fill a basket with fresh loaves of bread each morning, Marjorie Agosín survived her family's uprooting by gathering books. In "Words: A Basket of Love," she recalls how reading helped her to weather the lonely years of exile and discover her own vocation. While books by Gabriela Mistral and María Luisa Bombal taught her to entrust her innermost feelings of love and loss to paper, the young poet's devotion to Pablo Neruda was definitive. Indeed, even the structure of *The Alphabet in My Hands* recalls Neruda's *Confieso que he vivido* (1973), a series of autobiographical vignettes, each individually titled. Moreover, the intense love of Chile found in Neruda's autobiography informs Agosín's vision as well. The following passage from chapter 8 of *Confieso*, "My Country in Darkness," might well serve as an epigraph to *The Alphabet in My Hands*:

> I believe . . . the deracination of human beings leads to frustration, in one way or another obstructing the light of the soul. I can live only in my own country. I cannot live without having my feet and my hands on it and my ear against it, without feeling the movement of its waters and its shadows, without feeling my roots reach down into its soil for maternal nourishment.

Images of the poet in communion with the earth—the snow-covered landscape of New England, the red clay soil of Georgia, and the stones, shells, mosses, and mists of her beloved Chile—recur throughout Agosín's writings, as if handling, stirring, and caressing the earth will somehow unleash its benevolent, healing powers and make both the writer and the society whole again, beyond the pain of exile, beyond the loss of innocence.

Marjorie Agosín eventually traveled back to Chile for both personal and professional reasons. "Returns," the final chapter of this memoir, is devoted to joyful rediscoveries and the asking of terrible questions. As the jet transporting her and her children dances over the Atacama and the Andes on route to Santiago, the writer realizes that the familiar landscape she loves so deeply is nevertheless ablaze with horrors: "Why do I love this place that forced us into exile, that punished my father for being a Jew, that permitted the dismembered silence of the dead and the complicity of the living?" Accompanying a group of women to the northern deserts in search of their "disappeared," she understands that Chile, the country of her golden and blessed childhood, harbors secrets that must be told:

> They were good, these countrymen of mine. They were your brothers. Someone decided to blindfold them and take their lives. Someone decided they would not see another dawn, and that's what happened. The desert men died with their bodies underground, with murmurs of empty longings. They lived there for many days, forgotten, and the entire country refused to see them. But the desert cared for them, preserved their memory and that of the living.
>
> I return to the distant north, my forehead covered with saltpeter and the hardness of poor men. I also take with me the nation's open heart. All of Chile is a bleeding desert. Chile is the men found buried in the sand, and in the distance the accusing wind, the wind that tells all, and the sand a tender mother.

In his introduction to Maria Luisa Bombal's classic novella, *La última niebla* (1935), Spain's dean of literary scholars, Dámaso Alonso, praised the work as decidedly poetic and made special mention of Bombal's use of fog to represent the constant reverie into which her protagonist is plunged. Like Bombal, Marjorie Agosín often evokes the mists of Chilean streets and shores to weave the world of dreams and visions essential to her art. Many decades after he wrote it, Dámaso Alonso's assessment of Bombal's work captures the spirit of Agosín's current book:

> Reverie is the mediator, the medium or means by which dreams and reality are identified; it is the fog that erases, creates and fuses forms, wrapping them in its soft, fleecy mist. Reverie is not equivalent to what is dreamed or what is in truth lived; but, with its imaginative and sentimental flavor of memory and

hope, it has the virtue of maintaining, within that hermetic soul, a small window open to possibilities.

Memory, hope, and possibilities, the essential building blocks of Marjorie Agosín's poetic prose, are called forth in *The Alphabet in My Hands* to recreate a remarkable life, the story of a young girl, raised with love in the shadow of the Andes mountains, only to re-live, in her own way, the ancient diaspora of the Jewish people. From her adopted home in the United States, Marjorie Agosín writes to-day to recall the past, resist injustice, and reconcile us all to the joys and horrors of life in the twentieth century. Her book is indeed a window on the soul.

*Nancy Abraham Hall*

# The
## Alphabet
## in My Hands

# The Alphabet

*Beyond*
*the momentary*
*light*
*you were there, word,*
*mother tongue,*
*aroma,*
*dominion of memory.*

*I dreamed of inventing*
*your cadences,*
*rhythms tinged blue,* .
*like the color of certain replete*
*dreams.*
*I dreamed of the two of us,*
*and the alphabet burned with love.*
*At last I felt sated in my language,*
*secret, woven signs,*
*the illuminated manuscript*
*like the nights of the Jaguar.*

*Language,*
*alphabet in my hands,*
*I delighted in repetition,*
*blessed by sacred, melodious*
*discovery,*
*inhabited by pleasure.*
*Time and again*
*I repeated the words*
libélula
liturgia
litografía
literas

*I loved you totally,*
*I loved you rapturously,*
*I loved your nakedness,*

*the golden baroqueness of emotions,*
*small islands of translucent butterflies.*

*Mother tongue,*
*secret caress along the root*
*of my ear,*
*I who lack roots,*
*times, borders.*

*On the palate of that province*
*where all*
*dreams reside*
*I was an ancient, happy*
*child.*

*Suddenly*
*I felt the laments*
*of flight.*
*One mute night*
*I was taken from you,*
*left alone*
*without music*
*without bread,*
*an orphan*
*at a deserted table,*
*a vagabond*
*in countries without names.*

*They tore me from you, mother tongue.*
*I still feel that ferocious wound*
*unable to hear your*
*echo in my astonished ears*
*at dawn.*
*They took me far from you, mother tongue,*
*and my voice became a dormant candle.*

*Castillian tongue of mine,*
*you were not the language of my grandparents*
*but rather their consolation.*

*I miss you*
*and during nights of cloudy sorrow*
*I hear Helena's songs*
*in Sephardi*
*calling to me.*
*Little angel, little angel,*
*where have you gone, little angel?*
*Where have you gone, angel of my words?*
*Where have my mauve-colored verbs,*
*my discreet adjectives gone?*

*It is brutal to be another*
*in a different language,*
*forced into translation*
*and invented trajectories*
*to be unable to say, to be,*
*to not recognize*
*and always be asked*
*where are your parents from?*

*Mother tongue*
*I am censored,*
*without lips*
*nor seasons.*

*Beloved word of mine,*
*homeland of days and nights,*
*I want to embrace you*
*and stop your flight.*

*I lament vanished things,*
*thimbles, butterflies,*
*but most of all my mother tongue,*
*cut away in the midst of my life.*

*I lament not hearing you*
*in the morning*
*while you greet the women*
*and their brooms,*

*the children and their wide pockets,*
*the old women remembering yes,*
*the good old days were better.*

*Mother tongue,*
*come back to me,*
*awaken me.*
*I do not want to be a dry island,*
*I want to write along your arteries,*
*sail in your ship.*
*Wild and gentle language,*
*do not forget me.*

# Part 1

## childhood

# Chapter One

# *calendar*

## *Spring*

Spring returns to enumerate the cycles of the earth and summon the rhythm of words. Submerged, the earth awaits the spell of warmth in all its forms. How long have I lived in regions that do not belong to me? How do I remember the names of all the absences?

Sometimes I lean over to stir the soil. I am in the sinuous forests of Chile, the smell of eucalyptus settling along the length of my hands; at times it is the earth of Georgia, red like the happiness of a new life. Now I am in New England, awaiting another spring. The rains have passed and the birds return on bubbles of light. I, too , am here, but I return to memory. I am the sum of all the voyages and returns. I could no longer say that this is my place, that here I will plant trees. I can only promise that I will build a house full of words.

Suddenly the earth expands and folds. All the leaves of the earth are an alphabet in my hands. I remember my mother saying that we must water the earth and relieve the thirst of the dead. I lean still further over this damp, humid place and return to all the places I have been: the water, the highlands of Bolivia, the city of Santiago with its walls of smoke. And yet, my body has learned a new language, new sounds and cadences. Suddenly I recognize myself. I am from this place, I tell myself, and my hands open to receive the leaves that spell my name.

## Birth

During her fifth month, the doctors told my mother the baby she was carrying was dead. As she left the medical building, she plummeted into the sublime darkness of a mournful tunnel. The next day she returned to the office, and by one of those curious chances, the doctor decided to listen to me again. There I was. He recognized my heartbeat, and I slowly shifted, as through crystalline waters.

I was born during summer in the northern hemisphere, at dawn. They say I was fragile and bald for a year. My mother cried seeing me weak, barely able to enter life. Yet suddenly, when I knew I was alive in her arms, she said a reddish down began to cover my head, like a tenuous flame. Then someone told her I had been born under a lucky star, so they called me Marjorie Morningstar, after the girl in the Howard Fast novel, the television character "My Little Margie," and my Aunt Estrella who died in a concentration camp.

## Passover

The table as long as a map of distant lands spread before us children like a sovereign queen. Bouquets of white and mauve roses presided over the house, keeping the mirrors company, and my grandmother Helena, smiling and dancing, sliced apples into small pieces and mixed them with nuts. "This is Passover," she would say to me, "this is the holiday of freedom," and I assumed I could say forbidden words as well as polite ones, leave my hair uncombed, and lounge in a chair like a satisfied lady because that was happiness.

At Passover we sang and gossiped, whistled. From her kitchen of smoke and stars Carmencita sang the Ave Maria and made the sign of the cross for the sake of the heretics she served with love.

We felt less alone at Passover, the Haggadah contained illustrations similar to those in the books owned by the girls who lived at the corner. Everything about Passover had the fragrance of violets and then Easter week would arrive and we would eat fish from the Pacific that, like unleavened bread, had come from the heavens.

## Back to School

Along those coastal roads, the month of March would reinstate itself like the sovereign of drowsy days, days of fog, with a chill both tender and severe. Gone were the extended vacations when we women, sisters of summer, were always initiated into the rituals of desire. I remember the summer my mother first forbade us to wear tight white slacks and to stay on the beach for hours until the sand became the accomplice of our feet. But summer was also the future, the beginning of school, the new starched uniforms that seemed to belong to others. We loved to return to Santiago for Passover, the favorite holiday both in school and at my grandparents' house. I remember the four hundred chairs, one for each child, that we placed in the schoolyard for the festivities. On glorious, velvet afternoons touched by the still languid breezes of summer, we celebrated as the dazzling, stoic mountains of the Andes watched us break bread into small pieces. The earth smelled of stories, yet only in our imaginations did the river, pounding waves, and white slacks live on. I loved Passover for allowing me to tell the girls in my neighborhood that I, too, had angels who swooped over the homes of good Jews.

## March

When the southern hemisphere thinned its golden days and ushered in the season of returns, my sister and I dreamed of the day we would arrive in Santiago to buy material for our new uniforms. Each time we were lucky to obtain the latest silky cloth of cobalt and sky blue. Excited, we awaited our return to Santiago, to the structured days of that city of mountain chains and rubber plants. We liked to watch the clocks foretell our return to the predictable time when school began.

Then we went with our mother to buy material for our uniforms, pencils, school supplies, and lovely paper for covering our books.

But we were also sad because our old, worn uniforms would be handed down to María, who would mend and iron them for her own children and perhaps the children of others. Poverty was like that, mother said, and she told us about her own grandmothers and great-grandmothers who walked from Poland to Hamburg, then sailed on to Santiago de Chile. María, too, was like the women in my family, itinerant, nomadic, so sad in their silence, so meager in their poverty.

## The Blue Uniform

The uniform smelled of frost and starch. It rested in humble elegance across the chairs of the poor and the footrests of the rich. My uniform, resplendent, blue like a slice of fresh summer sky, or the praying shawls in which we hid when our grandfather blessed us. The skirt was very blue, the socks too white, the blouse the color of sandpaper, stiffened by a charcoal iron. Every morning the uniform shaped itself to my skin and pronounced the geography of my country. Children in southernmost Arauco wore it as did those in the north, and out in the streets, identically dressed, we recognized one another as fragile and vulnerable.

## My Apron

My apron was made of light percale cotton with patches of many colors, like the breath of peace. I loved my apron, protective fairy to the dark blue school uniform. The apron was a winter angel, a blanket of pale bluish snow on which to draw suns and myriad dreams. My mother had several aprons for each of us, a few for winter days with enormous, puffy cloudlike sleeves, good for stashing notes from admirers. The summer aprons were sown with flowers and fledgling orchards. They had two great pockets to which we entrusted our dreams and fondest desires, such as imagining the apron might rise into the sky and become a huge balloon in which to navigate the widest, bluest sky the earth had ever seen.

## My Desk

It was made of greenish mahogany. My mother says they brought it from the thick southern forests where gazes mingle with chloroform dreams and memory follows the rhythm of the rains. They say that two men had gone there to find it. My desk was green, noble, and hospitable, like the very tree that gave it life. From the time I was quite small I sat at my desk conversing with words. They were neither far nor near, yet they controlled me like voices from illuminated mirrors, like bonfires that left marks in the cup of my hands.

My mother gave me a key similar to those that fit the locks abandoned by my grandmother as she fled the weary streets and broken windowpanes of Vienna. I loved that key because it contained secrets as happy as the desire I felt whenever I prepared to sing or pray certain words. Inside my desk I kept eucalyptus leaves, fragrant as the deepest forest. I kept candelabras and seven candles, and the dreams of women who traveled to lands where nothing bloomed, of women who longed to be birds. Inside the green desk I kept my music, the music of the women I loved.

## Rabbit Easter

My aunt Liesl Goldschmid was born in Austria but was raised as an only child in London while her parents hid in the woods of Vienna. Like Agatha of Austria, she had the invincible custom of celebrating, year after year, the feast of the Rabbits. She said that Resurrection Sunday was a day for remembering those who were in hiding during the most treacherous years.

Very serious, she would create paths through the woods of the house next door, and sing Spanish songs while we hid multicolored eggs, painted lilac and mauve. In Chile, this was considered an act of bad faith, like the procession of heretics over the earth. Easter in Chile was subdued, and widows donned their most severe mourning clothes. That strange scene of Jewish children and their parents looking for eggs was not proper. But for us, the eggs hidden deep in the damp forest, and the sacred cheeks of those children, were like a beginning, the birth of innocence, of memory. We liked to hear my aunt proclaim "Oh, too much love," as she unpacked her wedding dress and danced in the transparent space of night and sea while we looked for eggs and buried our hands in the warm April earth, preparing ourselves for the southern hemisphere. We were happy because the previous week we had celebrated Passover as the maids watched us with surprise singing and repeating the questions of the night. Perhaps that was what it meant to be Jewish, to suffer the breath of God in the back of our necks while we prayed and to feel our hands buried in the soil while we looked for rabbits steeped in the wisdom of the earth.

## St. John's Eve

My nana Carmen Carrasco was a faithful observer of all manner of feast days, from the grape harvests on sweet and drowsy summer nights to the eve of St. John, her personal favorite. Carmen loved to dress in white so as to scare off Death and all her mischief making.

At midnight, the hour of owls and rivers—even though the one behind my house was merely a brook—Carmen went outside to beat the trees. She beat them in a marvelous frenzy, with all the fury of generations, with all the power of her womanhood. I watched her, wishing fervently to be grown up solely to beat trees, knowing full well that Jewish girls could never do so. We had no saint day's eves, no St. John.

On the nights she beat the trees, when her hair puffed up like a cloud of smoke, Carmen Carrasco took me to her room, yes, the room in the back, and told me the hour of my salvation had arrived. Since I was Jewish she baptized me with holy water brought from the fonts of nearby churches. She told me to stay very still so I wouldn't sprout horns. Only then did she tell me to look in the wide, concave mirror that would reveal a shift in my fortune. I was somewhere between subdued and happy, gazing into the mirror as if approaching the edge of a cliff, the cloudy ages of lost rituals, and I watched myself in the deep, transparent veil of this night of all nights. In the mirror, Carmen Carrasco saw the sinuous procession of the living and the dead, the stars of the most sublime galaxies. Carmen Carrasco assured me that the mirror told the truth. She whispered supplications, sweet prayers very close to my ear. She told me that she, too, was a Jewish woman, because, after all, the Spaniards were Jewish, and that, in order to survive, she had loved life above all else. This is how I spent my nights, my St. John eves, during winters in the southern hemisphere, when frost covered the fields of both rich and poor, when winter seemed like a great lady snug in her carriage of ice.

## My Birthday

Of all my memories, or what I choose to remember from among the mist and the moving boxes of forgetfulness, I remember my birthday celebrations. Nana Carmencha told me that mothers like mine did not give their babies names of saints or even have them baptized. That's why it was imperative to celebrate my birthday in the most baroque fashion possible. My nana Carmencha saw to it that birthdays took on the magic of a procession, by which she did not mean walking about with a saint on one's shoulders and genuflecting with thanks for a favor granted. Not that at all, but I will tell you that at seven in the morning, when the rebellious winter throws off its stubborn blankets, Carmen Carrasco and her helper Guillermina Oyarzún got up.

They lit the candles on an enormous, delicious cake, and aglow in their festive shawls, they went outside and walked around the block intoning "This is the morning song King David used to sing," then returned to our courtyard. I saw them through the misty windows, stunned with happiness to know that they had walked with a lit cake past the neighborhood butcher shop, the woman with the crooked mouth, and the knife-sharpener. They had blessed this saintless little girl's birthday.

Close behind them came my grandmother wearing the sky blue scarf that matched her eyes. Rather than cakes she brought a decapitated (and not very kosher) hen, a gift from Carmen's relative in Chillán. Upon seeing this pitiless animal, bathed in blood, I trembled, but knew that for the household servants, eating meat was the utmost pleasure. In the desolate countryside, hunger roamed the solitudes, so the hen was a celebration of abundance and good life.

During the day my mother prepared tirelessly for the celebration. She rushed off to the supermarket, or to Doña Jacinta's flower shop and returned with golden copihues. She and my grandmother then cut out the most beautifully colored paper shapes and created necklaces of marzipan. They peeled oranges and shaped the skins into little sailboats, and fashioned tiny dolls full of sugar with mirrors for faces. I watched them, but preferred to read my primer or talk to myself in the company of freshly sharpened pencils.

The adults arrived later, men in suits as dark as night and complexions yellowed by the exhaustion of avarice. Astonished, I watched them gesture as they conversed, weary and obedient to the rules of social obligation. They left gifts, plastic dolls, lavender water, a jar of peaches, a kilo of cheese, a secondhand book of drawings from my favorite uncle, and then they departed as hastily as they had arrived. In the interlude, my girlfriends convened. But I quickly tired of my peers. Pretending to have a terrible headache, I went to the attic where, behind a locked door, I waited for the guests to leave.

When the house returned to the peace of nightfall, when the evening noises turned to murmurs, I thought about my birthday party, the lit cake advancing along the street, my nana's prayers like sacred songs, and my grandmother parading through the neighborhood with the dead hen.

## Soledad

They had named her Soledad and her name prefigured a still body behind the ivy, small hands limply holding drab wild flowers, with the millenary tear that separates the healthy from the ill. Soledad had been born mentally retarded, her head somewhat bent and pointed, her drooping lips covered with reddish foam. In Chile, to be mentally retarded is not to exist, someone who must be hidden and who, by virtue of a vulnerable birth, is guilty. My parents wanted us to grow in compassion, in human solidarity, and so they spoke to us about Soledad, about the beauty of her amber-colored eyes, her hands desperate to catch the light. Every Sunday we walked to her house to play. We did not go to church or to synagogue because my father had told us that goodness exists on earth, that there were no rewards after death, and that playing with Soledad was a mitzvah. A mitzvah was not repaid with either chocolates or eternal life. Rather, it was like writing a poem, always immediate, timeless, and beautiful. There was something very direct in any conversation with Soledad, and we played with her bald dolls. Soledad pulled their hair out in order to cover them with it. From time to time happiness invaded her knees and, with all the noise of the sea, she asked us to dance the Twist, getting to her feet like a comet, smiling. We hugged Soledad and thought about Gabriela Mistral's poems. It was true that as we danced we were queens and the garden filled with shadows and lanterns, and we danced without speaking or moving. We danced because our hearts were bleeding life, because on that Sunday afternoon Soledad was not alone, and her solitude had become a basket full of smiles.

## Rain

The rain was not a merciful blanket of water descending from the sky. The rain was angry, sweeping away the humble table, the fragile roofs of tin and cardboard. The rain arrived in the immenseness of night, as if death had arrived, inopportune, without warning. The children who shielded themselves with pieces of cardboard became covered with malign water that kept them awake even more than their hollow dreams, more than the impudent immediacy of hunger. Over there, in the other Chile, the rain danced on huge windows and the children in those neighborhoods, including myself, ate toast and drank hot chocolate. The grown-ups declared the storm to be beautiful and admired the savage flames in the fireplace. The rain, too, was poverty's enemy. With indifference, she swept away the tiny, frail, makeshift huts, refuges for poor and rich alike.

## The Beggar Woman

It is hard to see how big or small she is. Kneeling, she seems as fragile as drizzle. She has as many names as corners, but at night, when she shelters herself from sadness in a shawl as changing as clouds, her name is Magda. I see her every day shaking her small tin can, making music with simple coins. She makes her rounds in the morning. She begs for money and she prays. At times she sings certain passages from the Bible, but she gets them wrong because her memory is failing. Later, when the noonday sun warms her, Magda, who is also Mary, returns to collect litter and discarded bottles for resale.

I stop to speak to her. She waits for me as our meetings have become routine. Sometimes I bring her paper cut in the shape of stars or the sun, and she is delighted. She asks me where I live, if my house is close by. She says she lives down south, far away, where the wind noisily attacks rooftops and splits her long, black, hand-me-down skirt.

My grandmother says that one shouldn't speak to the poor, or worse, pay them any attention. Besides, she doesn't even hear me. I keep telling Magda that tomorrow I will bring her more paper stars, and I return to my warm bed and try to imagine Magda's face, which does not exist, which I cannot recall as vividly as her poverty and her tattered black shawls.

## Long Live Saint Peter!

All night long the women of the village took care of him. They rubbed his wooden body with branches of eucalyptus and spring flowers like lilies and forget-me-nots. Quiet peace emanated from his body, and around him, the bonfires burned like transparent circles of light and the blood of so humble a heart. "Long live Saint Peter!" they said to him, and a chorus, bowing in the thick night and drinking grape brandy, said "Long live! Long live!" My mother took us to see the saint as well, and we touched his body covered with branches and flowers, just as earlier, on those March days, we had touched and kissed the Torah. Faith seemed like those blue shawls my grandfather donned to pray. Faith seemed like the destiny of a restless, shifting sea assailing us.

Very early in the morning, when the sea descended angrily on the sand and the night ceded its realm to the still fragile blinks of the morning sun, the fishermen left their brightly colored houses. They wore wool caps made by their wives and they left on boats named for flowers and lovers: "María Celeste," "Rosa de la Costa," "María del Valle Azul," and the saint would rock, guiding them with his blind, doubtful faith, with his wooden torso ringed with flowers. Meanwhile we were there, on the side, along the shoreline, lighting small candles of love, strewing rose petals into the water so that the saint would have a fragrant journey. It was then that I realized it didn't matter whether we were Jewish or Catholic, the most important thing was faith. Here it was like a double flame of love and peace; here we were, young Jewish girls, keeping St. Peter company and then following the Belgian priest to Mass at the small stone church, the church where the poor illuminated the earth and the priest said, with a French accent, "Long live Saint Peter! Long live God and the Virgin Mary!" We were happy because in that procession of acquaintances and strangers we did not feel alone. No one spit at us like the well-brought-up British schoolgirls. This was the real Chile: a chain of good men and women whose beloved Saint Peter, the miraculous saint of the sea, reddened by rings of roses, disappeared and then reappeared over the horizon of faith.

## September 18

The women of the house spoke about September 18. They intoned strange sentences. Some said tiki, tiki, tik, and moved their feet as if they might be swept, dancing, to the ends of the earth. My mother smiled as well and said tiki, tiki, tik. The 18th was a patriotic holiday in this odd nation that celebrated the days on which battles had been lost, and whose national hero was a blue-bearded Irishman. My mother said that this holiday was very important for the goyim, the non-Jews, just as the New Year was for us. From that moment on, I knew we were half Chilean and half Jewish.

For me the 18th marked the invasion of our garden by wild aromas: wisteria and gum trees germinated, certain warm and reddish roses bloomed. The 18th was like spring with weeping willows sighing and dancing. On that day my nana dressed me in layers of petticoats, like a cabbage, and put red and white ribbons, the colors of the flag, in our hair. Generally we spent the holiday at the beach house. Nana took me to the Arbors, a group of small straw cabins that brought to my mind the *sukka* of the Jewish people. In the Arbors men and women danced, got drunk, fell in love. The women, with unhurried grace, lifted their skirts and looked at one another, then chose partners for the night. The smell of pine and blue sea blended with the melodious waves, with the movement of bodies, with the to and fro of the breeze and of love. Even though they said this holiday was not ours, I loved it just the same, tied to my nana's arm, that dark and noble arm that cured fevers and placed white calyxes in my ear. I, too, went to dance among the people they called poor and lazy Indians.

My people were somber and danced only on the 18th. Even so, they danced slowly, their heads hanging slightly. They asked forgiveness, and they gave themselves the luxury of getting drunk once a year, in September, so to honor a country that viewed them with indifference and arrogance.

My grandfather died on September 18, our nation's special day. They transported him to the Jewish cemetery of Santiago where all the workers stood with their red and white flags among the headstones etched with Hebrew letters. On each small stone there was a flag. Then and there I knew that Chile was ours as much as its air, its garbage, and its dead.

## The Marconi Theater

My grandmother was afraid of prayers, but she warbled like a lovestruck bird. She always said that the real paradise was here on earth, and that was why I loved her, because she was mischievous and disorderly, because she read love letters out loud. On fast days, she used to become annoyed at all the the gods, banners, and Carmen's Virgin. As if pleasantly drunk, she ate ham and fried fish with exquisite indifference. My grandfather would say, "You ought to be ashamed, Josefina, on the holy days." She would look at him unmoved and continue savoring the sweet taste of her forbidden dinners.

I, on the other hand, would draw near to grandfather, stealing my small hand into his enormous green coat, and get ready to go out with him to the Marconi Theater, where the German Jews celebrated the holy days. My grandfather and I most often took a taxi and had the driver drop us off five blocks before the theater so that everyone else would think we had arrived on foot. I liked to lie about such things because they were delicious and impressive lies, lies that adults told, not children.

We would arrive at the Marconi Theater where the men smelled of confinement and bygone ages. These men greeted my grandfather in German, and he was thrilled to hear his own language. His language? The language that killed millions of Jews, but he was happy with so little. That was my grandfather, too good to be human. They called him "the angel." I would sit on his lap trembling with song and prayer. I am sure that he thought of his father in his solitary tomb in the woods of Vienna, and he would beat his breast and pray for the angels, for the sparrows, for all his beloved dead, numbering more than six million, and for the Jews, who were acknowledged only on feast days.

My grandfather was like a resting place. His was the grace and gift of the enlightened, and I loved him and prayed for his dead in that Marconi Theater. Between prayers the afternoon passed slowly, like random, rainy days. We, the little Jewish girls, winked at one another. Perched on our grandfathers' laps, we exchanged sweets, orange blossoms, the pleasing things of happiness. My grandfather would beat his breast and kiss me. We would go to a place beyond time, and the men and women would hug and say in German "Alles Gute, alles Schöne." I would also repeat those words in that language, which sounded wild to me, and feeling wild and dark myself, I yearned to go tell Carmencita that I was surely seated among her saints and braziers.

## Rosh Hashanah

October in Chile is warm. The inhabitants take off their endless layers of scarves and excite to the explosion of greens and yellows. It is the season of aromas. Life is pursued. Retired people return to the spots that have been held for them. After a dark winter, balloons appear, morning glories, violets, caresses in the park. Cemeteries fill with flowers that always accompany the dead.

October in Chile, and it is the Jewish New Year, even though few people know it, and at times people in the street simply say that the Jews have closed their shops. My mother and I look at one another with delight, we laugh with such passion because we don't know what to say. We were bending over with laughter and also with humility and we were getting ready to celebrate this new year which, more than a fresh start on a calendar, marks a different way of viewing the world and becoming accustomed to it. Perhaps the Jewish New Year is a way of accepting time. Entangled and enormous, time is like a stellar shawl, like a time beyond our grasp, a useless time, and as such, a time submerged in otherness. My mother tells me to collect stones so that we can throw them in the river and ask for forgiveness. I tell her that there aren't many sins I can recall. Perhaps when I pulled my sister's hair, but most of all I just remember bits of scenes, intermittent and forgotten memory.

The Jewish New Year, and the ten days that surround it, is a time not only of introspection but of gratitude beyond alphabets and calendars, beyond thresholds and uncertain times. My grandfather would take me to the Sephardic synagogue because he felt at home there. It was, in truth, a great theater with reddish, dragon-like rugs leased by Jews from the capital and the provinces. They got together on these holy days. We walked enveiled in the smell of hyacinths, the light of spring glowing on our faces full of yearning. At last we had a holiday! Since I was little, strolling arm in arm with my grandfather, we spoke about how hardheaded God was with regard to the poor, about how the Andes looked like an enormous Chantilly cream pie. More than anything, I remember the Sephardic community gathering in the streets near the synagogue, smiling, singing with whistles and drums Old Castillian and gypsy melodies, and we, the *Kulturmenschen*, would walk austerely, germanically, to pray to a silent uncaring God who let millions die in the chambers of blue gas. My Omama Helena sent me a disapproving glance because she saw the questions in my eyes. She taught me to remain quiet in the face of the incomprehensible, the inexpressible. From that Jewish New Year on, I entered into an eternal conflict with God, and it was not just a passing phase of adolescence. I understood that religious knowledge goes beyond history, beyond books of fiction. It is a way to contemplate the sky, to approach the time of breezes, to embrace the beggars, and to go wherever our hearts may lead us.

## Kol Nidre

It was the most wondrous night of nights. The moon above the sky's open labyrinth lit the path of silence on this night of wonders, on this night when grown men repent, beat their breasts, and repeat words as if praying or moaning, "Mea culpa, mea culpa."

A woman seated beside us searches for her dead sisters in the melodies of Kol Nidre. She also looks for herself, bewitched by the horror, and she sings like an angel, her throat full of mist. Her voice is unrepentant, yet it murmurs: I seek the water of the living in the grottos of the dead.

My mother winks at me and says she is not sorry about anything. She has not sinned, she says. She has only played with the afternoon, with the leaves, and has marveled at the lavishness of leisure. She has stored her shoes with the somnolent autumn leaves and has visited the sick without offering false hope. I see her as if she were floating, green from head to toe, in a spiral of smoke, far from those men who beat their breasts and then yell over money or unrequited love.

In the distance I hear a woman sobbing, her voice a dry violin in all the deserts of the world. This is the night of Kol Nidre, the most wondrous night, the most wary night, the night of those who repent.

## Day of Atonement

We liked the Day of Atonement because we felt closer to the girls in our neighborhood who, every Sunday, disguised as starch, went to speak to the parish priest in those marvelous velvet rooms where one knelt to tell secrets about touching one's body in the resplendent solitude of night and yelling obscene words for the sheer pleasure of how it feels to stroke one's belly at the sound of them. But to whom could we confess about how bad we had been or how many dirty words we had said? Our family had few prohibitions. The Day of Atonement drew us closer to the Christian girls we so wanted to be like, girls with holy cards, First Communion girls. My mother didn't like to go to God's house where men beat their breasts then put their hands in their pockets to count money. None of that, my mother would say. So we would go to the river, dressed in white and carrying lilies. We washed our hair and looked for fresh stones. We threw the stones into the river with love, stones like prayers. The stones were for our sins, for the times we had disobeyed, been stubborn, wished for bad things to happen. We threw a lot of stones. We liked the sound they made, and we liked knowing that the turbulent, crystalline river, slippery as bubbles, swept away our sins and evil deeds. Later that afternoon we felt happy and light. God's house was everywhere, especially in my mother's hands that gently caressed us. That's how we celebrated the Day of Atonement.

## Christmas Eve at the Pacific

At night the ocean became thin and sighed in preparation for the days of perpetual sun and water. I loved Christmas as something forbidden, something that I could never have. My grandfather said that Christmas was like the mouth of the night, very dark for Jews. My grandmother, in a wise and distant voice, replied that all nights were dark for Jews. For a long time I did not understand when people said to me, "You Jews killed Christ," and "You Jews are strange, " and "You Jews do not celebrate death as we do." On Christmas Eve, when the nanas put on their best clothes and placed clay pitchers in every corner, I felt distant and alone. Being Jewish was like having an open wound that never healed.

One Christmas my nana Delfina saw me sobbing in the shadows and she said, "Dry your tears, little girl, and let's go dancing." Together we joined the crowd that had gathered outside to celebrate the birth of the Christ child. Nana bought me a beautiful bouquet of red carnations and parsley for good luck. And when no one was looking, she opened her patent leather wallet and gave me the best Christmas present I have ever received: a small Star of David as golden as my hair.

## New Year's by the Sea

New Year's is celebrated by the sea, in the disorderly, uncombed city of Valparaíso, where sky and sea blend under colored lanterns hung high in the Pacific night. An ancient pyrotechnic tradition, more or less a hundred years old, is the pride of a city that was first among Pacific ports during the previous century.

Today the inhabitants of Valparaíso don their garments of poverty, and still transport water on exhausted mules laden with garlands of flowers, mules that also obey misery's avatar. The whorehouses of the city, where naked, impoverished sailors turn love's pirouettes, are also illuminated majestically. Ladies of the night, painted red and in fuchsia high heels, head for the docks, aroused.

Every corner and hill is occupied by anxious spectators who, since dawn, have made the blue pilgrimage to claim their place near the sky. The balconies of the poor are cleared tonight of the usual washing hung out to dry and allow an unimpeded view of the bursts of happiness and the sea, with its ancient, defeated ships of war: the *Esmeralda*, the oldest ship in the Chilean fleet, sailing the world displaying her white magic riggings.

Suddenly in the sea and sky, the night wind flares into a single flame of air and light. Life and death, dreams of the future, what will and cannot be, strike an agreement on this night by the sea. Strangers hug as if the world's end had come. They dance barefoot along the tree-lined avenue, along Lovers' Way, and even stutterers sing. On this beloved night, one of few that Chileans recognize as their own, golden stars and old women on balconies, above the crowds and the ashes, launch warm, blue doves into the hills.

## Summers of Syrup

Summers were spreading like golden lizards from early December to mid-March. Beach days drew near and we entered the space of happiness. We finished the school year. My mother, who, like her mother, feared rickets above all other diseases, prepared us for a luminous pilgrimage to the coast. The car was loaded with matresses, blankets, jars of sugar, peaches, and tuna fish. We began our journey along the sinuous highways as if we were traveling to the end of the earth. In truth the coast was quite nearby, only an hour and a half from the capital. A good part of the ritual involved the food supply and the obligatory escape of the melon, rolling off ceremoniously each time we climbed a hill. My mother, resembling a victorious bird, watched over the stash of small lemons.

I cannot clearly remember precise moments, dates, or events, but happiness was an outstretched hand, an open handkerchief, something fleeting and intangible, yet at the same time present and real. Never again have I been able to recover this feeling. The summer consisted of nights turning into day and days into night. Rushing was unheard of and in bad taste. We were not lazy. Rather, time took on a different rhythm, measured by a different gauge. Haste was looked at askance because one had to pause in the hearts of flowers, look at tiny dragonflies, the night rain on the cacti, or red leaves that had been well preserved since the previous autumn.

We went on long afternoon walks on a steep earthen path along enormous cliffs. The rocks took the shape of legends, their faces sculpted by the wind and the imagination. My mother often took us to the Princess Rock with the face of a woman in love, her eyes turned inward. She told us that the Princess cried, especially when the moon was full, because she was in love with the sea.

Everything by the sea took on the organic rhythm of life: the tides rested and dreamed, the footsteps galloped after the sand, the house recovered light and a face in the morning, and opened itself religiously at noon. It was probably in this small stone house by the sea that I first felt the shudder at the sound of poetry, communion with the living and the dead, the aroma of Doña Blanquita's freshly baked bread, and the antics of the inebriated men on the corner. But nothing seemed out of kilter. Everything in that dominion, from the smallest to most gigantic thing, had its peculiar essence, its own gestures. All one had to do was watch and interpret the watery movements of the lizards, the nuns resting in the blue kitchen, the crabs kicking in the fish market stalls. It all signaled you were alive.

## Tidal Pools

Every summer we went to the shore, time set aside for wandering along the sonorous, silent sand. Every summer we walked by the sea, along the beach, as if caressing the body of someone we love. My childhood transpired in the small coastal town called El Quisco. Due to frequent blackouts in the village, electric light was scarce at night. Potable water was also scarce. Each house had its own septic well, and we spent hours pumping. Flies appeared like privileged guests in the blue kitchen during light meals, and yet, we were happy, caught in the languid rhythm of each day's passing, in the beauty of an unexpectedly slow day, the sound of the ocean and its fragrances. At night my sister and I read poems by Gabriela Mistral and dreamed we were queens.

In El Quisco I lived alongside fishermen and breadmakers, and the area's intellectuals who left behind the impetuous rush of normal days and elected barefoot time in the sand, the peace that allowed them to welcome angels and converse with the living.

Summers at water's edge allowed me deeper knowledge of my own body, which in many ways became waterlike. My form stretched and my hair became tangled in seaweed. Water ran down my legs, just as the tiny stream of blood had done when I turned thirteen. Water made me feel alone, free of other people, of the gaze of villagers who said: Those summer people, those blonde foreigners should arrive any day. The sound of men's whistling voices did not upset me when I was at the tidal pools. There I felt happy because the water was like fog, like cloudy crystals, and my body, which needed no reply, was just there, the way things are, day and night.

## Gypsy Women

In summer, when days grow as long as patience, we used to go to the plazas to see the gypsy women arrive. There they were, in the wake of winter's shadows, with their tents like secrets and moist palaces. There they were with their silk skirts, withered by the clouded gaze of passion and badly plotted secrets. They seemed to float among the shrubs, walk across forbidden lawns, go off in bare feet to urinate like an orchestra of crickets. Sometimes their clothing would not cover their private parts, and everyone stared at them, especially at the clusters of hair between their legs. Then we saw her approaching us. Her hands were the size of storks, and she said, "Bonfires bloom in your heart." Gypsy women asked for nothing, only the gold coins that pedestrians generously tossed at them in every neighborhood.

At first I was afraid of them because the maids at my house insisted they would kidnap me, drag me to a dark hallway, and cut out my heart. Little by little I began to love them unreservedly like the noise of dreams. Every summer when I was allowed to bare my legs and feel the yearning presence of desire, skin shedding its petals, I invoked their image. Then we went out into the plaza and saw them in their crazy witches' garments, bunches of silk at their hearts, and they would say to me, "My darling girl, give me your hand." I gave them my hand because I was alone, because I was like them. I, too, had come out of my dark castle. I gave them my hand, some jewelry that I received from a few dark ancestors. In the end I offered them both hands, faintly lined and ripe for invention. I gave them my faith and asked in exchange that they caress my palms.

## The Movies

Adolescence emerges from the shadows and the face of the girl I was comes into view. The past is an uncertain braid. I remember going often with my mother to a small movie theater. Located in the beach town of El Quisco and painted cobalt blue and turquoise, it stood on a rocky, dusty corner reminiscent of those ghostly towns in northern Chile where men lose their way in the fog and women become lost in their houses. Around seven in the evening, I thrilled to hear my mother say she wanted to go into town to watch the sunset and later a film. There were no rules, as there were in the cities, about how old one had to be to enter the theater. There were no absurd ratings pronouncing "age fourteen and up only."

So we put on our white slacks and went to the movies, where there were no orchestra or box seats, only wooden chairs carved from familiar trees. We sat with our snacks, bananas and milk for me and lots of strong coffee for my mother. We also brought along candies to share with whoever happened to sit next to us. Attending a movie in that beach town felt like communal living. There were no distinctions between rich and poor, summer residents and natives. In certain ways the movies, like school uniforms, made us feel equal, like a family, accomplices in that world of illusion up on the screen. I loved to hear people say that my golden hair reminded them of Marilyn Monroe's.

## The Island of Swallows

During the summer, when nights weighed little and sadness was warm and fleeting, I liked to tie myself to my mother's body, sense her jasmine smell, slide my hand through her curls, imagining them to be copper-colored waves. That's how we spent the summer, next to one another, asleep in the wondrous stupor of days that repeated themselves, equal in their slowness, in their rhythm of chance and sand games. Then, so as not to alter the habit of repetition, I asked my mother to tell me the story of the Island of Swallows.

As she spoke, she ran her hands through my hair: One summer there was a girl who dreamed about swallows. She played in her garden beside the woods, at once far from and close to the sea, and dreamed about swallows, like angels with white breasts plowing the domed sky. Then suddenly, she felt herself being lifted like a blue snowflake, her body like a luminous summer wing. The swallows were taking her to an island where the sea was full of anemones, wisteria, and small flowers, where the sea was a blue and violet gauze.

It was their island, a place where naked women combed their hair and fastened their curls with combs of generous wood. On the Island of Swallows words danced beside the women. The only sound came from the gentle, prodigious cadence of words traversing the sky. The women told one another stories, and whenever their spirits or words ran low, the swallows helped them out. Then I looked at my mother with delight, because I realized that on the Island of Swallows there were no dark words, memories were the color of turquoise, and words bloomed in the water like magic trees. I always wanted to live on the Island of Swallows. There the dead would appear dancing on the foliage sparkling with ashes. Now they spoke to those women who had perished in the forests of ash. Now they spoke with languages of water and fire. I understood that on the Island of Swallows memory was allowed, that only there could I emerge from the shadows and be happy amid faith and words.

In the dense nights, when the soul is an agile feather, I return to the Island of Swallows. There I find my mother, her fingers like pencils floating in the sand. I stand at her side on an island where pilgrims rest and the sea is a thick waist in the rhythm of the night. Suddenly the swallows appear, surrounding my head. Enamored of these nighttime birds and their flight, I open and shut my eyes, and know myself to be at the heart of memory, in a childhood amid forests and fresh, sonorous water. I lie naked next to my mother and write a story about a girl who grows up on the Island of Swallows, an island built on memories that plow the nights and clear the days. My mother now asks me to tell her about the Island of Swallows, and when I cannot get to sleep, I take her hand. My copper-colored hair blends with hers and I say, "Mom, once upon a time there was an island inhabited by swallows . . . ," and we set out for the world of words.

## Guardian Angels

Summers were always spent by the sea, beyond the hills. From every corner of the house it was possible to catch a glance of the ocean, which neither lurked nor asked questions. The sea was one of those vulnerable presences, it had roots and awoke in love with it's own waves. At night the sea undulated in the wind, in the air, its waters rocking like a magic seesaw.

I grew up by the sea and believed in all the tales of her islands and archipelagos because my country was entwined with the ocean everywhere. Sometimes its enveloping presence blinded us or made us unhappy.

Life in the summer was water, sunsets, sand, walks to the Princess Rock and back to the house after dark, down the dirt road where not even the vast silence terrified us.

At summer's end, so-called soirées were celebrated at water's edge. They consisted of carnival acts with midgets and disobedient girls. My mother took us to those festivities. I loved the beach late at night and the huge bonfires. My hair was grown long and I was dressed in white, as I had always dreamed. Led along by my older sister, I caught a first glimpse of lovemaking and desire.

On the last night of that week by the sea, Antoine de Saint-Exupéry's incredible story *The Little Prince* was enacted. The insinuating fox appeared, full of maleficent weaknesses, the fox that made us tremble, she was so astute. Suddenly the lights on the beach went out. The water seemed frozen in place and the ocean turned very thick. There was no moon that night, no wind, only the fragrance of forests and lavender. Then out on the immense expanse of the Pacific a boat appeared, draped in white sails, like a mirror. It came to take the Little Prince away so that he would not be tempted by the fox, and took him to another island where he would likely live with his rose, surrounded by water and beauty.

I understood then that perhaps we all had many guardian angels, that at the decisive moment someone ultimately looks out for us. The day we left Chile I thought of the plane as the boat that had taken the Little Prince to new waters. Then I prayed for what I was leaving behind and what the future might hold. My breathing marked the rhythm of the engines as on the night when I felt my heart to be a single watery wave. I held my mother's hand, closed my eyes, and remembered an entire childhood by the sea in my house of stone.

# Chapter Two

# *Being Jewish*

Living among pious churchgoers, left- and right-wing Catholics, who were we? How did we see ourselves as they prepared for Holy Week and the streets became precipices streaming with flying banners? Many times, from the vantage point of maturity, I have asked myself what it meant to be a Jew in Chile, to grow up Jewish among saints, First Communions, and Mays devoted to the worship of the Virgin Mary.

To be Jewish in Chile was to be above all a foreigner, the girl who at times, in dreams, sprouted horns, the girl who could never eat ham. Whenever she was invited to lunch, they asked, perversely, is it true that you don't eat ham?

To be Jewish in Chile was to be an intruder, a guest who spoke the same language, went to the same school, played hopscotch, but was nevertheless strange, ugly, big-nosed. Others were also strange: the Italians, the Arabs, the French, but they were more Chilean than we. Something unfathomable made us feel radically different, and although they never spat at me, and did not openly despise me, I carried inside a well-hidden sense of yearning like the slow agony of the marked. That agony flowed toward my skin each time my friends' parents asked me about the land of Israel, a place I had never seen, each time they asked me when I would go to Europe, the land of my great-grandmother Helena, I would tremble and hear only the trains in the darkness, the time of terror reflected behind her frozen expression. In such moments I did not want to know who I was, nor what it meant to be a Chilean Jew. I wanted only to run away and to rest my head against my mother's lips.

## Arrivals

Many of them arrived with glazed eyes and pain on their faces. After storms at sea aboard wailing boats, they caught sight of the coastline, of the sun gone mad in all its radiance. They heard and saw unknown birds and luxuriant yellow flowers. The water was like words of love and desire. Jews arrived on Latin America's Atlantic and Pacific shores, and the pain—of the ineffable, the pointlessly violent firestorm—began to subside and take the form of light. This was Latin America, not its northern counterpart. It was a weak, impoverished America, yet a generous one where refugees found shelter among the many and were not singled out as strangers. They were simply there, living in these lands, in cities that had nothing to do with the ones they had left behind. The new cities were now theirs forever. Jews knew that they would never have to leave America in search of other lands or seas. America was the only possible route, and here they would stay amidst the rain forests, tangles of wild birds, astounding blizzards, and the warm welcome of the Andes Mountains.

Jews in America learned to love these poor, soulful countries without a future. They learned the customs of love and conversed with the women who sold herbs. They settled in colorful neighborhoods, sang nostalgic ballads, and in return heard *rancheras, cuecas*, and *tonadas*. I loved Chile above all else and still claim to be part of this America, the one that dreams in Spanish, even though its students, my peers, glory and peace of the land, addressed me as you, the Jews. When all was said and done, I felt a part of them, I felt I belonged. I liked to say hello to the herb vendor and the man sharpening kitchen knives on the sidewalk in the morning. I loved to kiss the hand of Doña Eduvigis, healer of bad dreams and upset stomachs.

In South America we lit candles every Friday night to bring peace to our dreams and lives. Every Sunday we woke to the rhythms of happiness because the nuns who taught school and the women who lived on the corner passed our house on their way to church, to pray just as we did on Saturdays.

On the other hand, Jews in North America are not very much like me. They are Jewish North Americans. Their America belongs to them. We Jews in Latin America remain always grateful for the ports of entry opened to us, yet underneath the bed we always keep a suitcase.

## Names

My name. So many times they ask me about it. Marjorie, I tell them. With a *j* or a *g*? It doesn't matter, I say. Then another question. Is your name Margarita? No, I tell them. I was born here, in North America, and my name is Marjorie Morningstar. Morningstar? Like the Jewish girl in the book? But you're not Jewish! Yes, I tell them, on both sides. My mother and father, my grandparents and great-grandparents. It seems strange to them. You don't look Jewish, they say. There are Jews in Chile? Yes, I tell them, almost twenty thousand.

They say nothing at first, then they repeat that I seem odd to them, not like the Jews of North America who own all the newspapers and magazines. No, I tell them, the Jews of Chile are more or less poor.

What is your name? They ask me again, and I repeat it once more, each distinct syllable. It will invent a history for me, as if each word were returning to another frontier, to latitudes that no longer belong to me. And I want to go back, run, retreat, find my nana, bury my face in her fruit-stained apron. I want to find her, as I did on those days when they would say: "There goes the Jewish girl. What a shame! She is so pretty."

What is your name? This time I tell them my name is María Santa Cruz.

## Last Names

What is your last name, my child? Where do you live? Which nuns are your teachers? I did not have a distinguished or wealthy last name. Indeed, my father wasn't even sure that we were Agosíns. Our name was lost in the course of so many pilgrimages and flights. Neither estate nor vineyard owners, we lacked the appropriate pedigree, and certainly no Jewish children were allowed into the Catholic schools, not even in disguise. Our saving grace was that we did not "look Chilean," which meant that we were not Indian, or perhaps Spanish in appearance. We were pale, very pale, our eyes blue. We were Jewish, but not obviously so, according to our own maids and those in the neighborhood. Even though we were Jewish and our belongings were shabby, we didn't look Indian, and in Chile that meant a lot.

## The Goyim

Anybody who was not Jewish like us, my grandfather called Goy. They in turn called us Poles. In other words, all Jews from White Russia were Poles, and Sephardic Jews were Turks. The Turks, according to my grandmother Josefina, ran small retail shops, and every afternoon we walked to the Turk's shop, even though he wasn't from Turkey, but Palestine.

That's what it was like, being a foreigner in Chile. We had names, but in general they were inaccurate. I noticed that Goyim always kissed each other out of doors, with innocence, resplendently, and sometimes clapped their hands upon seeing a beautiful woman walk by. They would summon me—"Come here, little Pole"—and braid my hair and sing me very beautiful Spanish songs, like succulent magic threads.

When I feel sad, or watch films about Jews in the gas chambers, I think about the Goyim of my childhood. I think about how happy they were, especially after banquets at which they had consumed, they assured me, an entire roast pig, legs and all, plus a huge jug of wine, then slept forever and a night. I know that they would not have killed me, nor shaved my head. They would not have laughed at me.

## Being Jewish

We lived in a middle-class neighborhood that had previously been one of the most elegant in Santiago. I played with the neighborhood children, the Mellao sisters who loved me and called me *porotito*, that is, "little bean," because I was small for my age. I attended neither the public school nor the private one in our neighborhood. They said I went to the school for Israeli girls because they were afraid to say the word Jewish, as if it were a wound or a wild, irate insult. I did not see myself as an outsider, yet I felt different, despite the blue uniform all schoolgirls wore. I was Jewish. The maids sometimes told me so, and occasionally someone would spit as we walked by. Once, on a trip to Southern Chile, I saw German settlers spit at a group of short, gray Chileans. I realized then, that I, too, occupied a strange place within the racial scheme of things. Neither Spanish, nor Indian, nor a mixture of the two, I was not American, but foreign. I ate unusual meals, and learned an odd language at school. Always the other, always translated. Perhaps that is what being Jewish means: suffering from a chronic illness. Yet I was only mildly conscious of my condition, and rarely gave it much thought. I was a Jew in Chile, and being Jewish made me neither more nor less happy until the day I traveled north to Chacabuco. There I met the concentration camp guard, and I told him, Sir, I am Jewish. And he kissed my hand. At that instant I knew myself to be truly a Jew.

## Religious Education

At our tiny elementary school, a private British academy for children of the well-to-do and self-important, being Jewish manifested itself in signs of strangeness. For example, whenever we were offered a ham sandwich, we had to say "No, thank you, my religion doesn't allow it." Or when the teacher asked us if we had antique silver candlesticks at home, the sort whose crackled surfaces seemed to have come from the bottom of the sea, I said yes. But the candlesticks she had in mind were those displayed in honor of Mary during her special month, and I barely knew who Mary was.

These always-present differences marked the rhythm of my childhood. More than anything else, we felt what it meant to be Jewish on those days when religious education classes were held. Holding hands two by two, the students filed across the school patio, while my sister and I were left stranded, two girls in an empty play yard fenced by solitude. The others looked at us with subtle smiles, silently taking in the perverse and frightening nature of our difference. They watched us as if we were trapped, with nowhere to run or to hide.

I stared at the trees and pretended they were parting for us, when in truth there was no escaping those moments of infamy. Through what door, over what threshold of dreams could we go to our own religion class where the Star of David would not have to be hidden? There we sat, as if in a strange time, a time devoid of audacity and reverence. We were and we were not refugees, classmates at a school for wealthy little girls, those upper-class children who viewed us with hatred because we were Jews. And we remained alone. And we did not know whether we were real or merely the dream of those who had never been foreigners.

## Frida and Moisés

They are both short and time has bestowed on them a sense of grace and peace. They have a close likeness, as couples do whose love is deep and lasting. They are my parents. I see them walking under an immense blue umbrella, and I am afraid that they will be lifted into the air, leaving me alone on the earth. Life without them is inconceivable to me, because even grown children suffer the anguish of their childhoods, of noises in the night, of empty rooms that are besieged by pain.

They walk along the grass. The umbrella envelopes them like the shawl worn in God's house. Their faces and eyes seem to belong to the blue and greenish stars and the rain that lengthens their feet.

How I love them, and how vivid the memory of their stories, my father's tales about butterflies and their destinies, my mother's accounts of African princesses. At night I only have to close my eyes to see them next to my bed, their sweet-smelling bodies exuding tenderness. Then, I summon sleep. I pray for them in the language of peace and say, "May God protect all parents so that the orphans of the earth may stop death in its tracks. May God protect those children who, without parents, will not be recognized in this world."

## Sundays

It was always Sunday when stars and kites of many colors appeared in the streets. My parents would get up very early. I sensed them in the warmth of their murmurs, in the peace of those who walk together, who somehow become accustomed to permanence, and through life's synchronies, become alike. That's how my parents were. They got ready to go out to vote, he wearing his best blue suit and she her best dressy white blouse, because voting in Chile was something joyous. They held hands along the immense avenue lined with wide-topped trees, and all the flags at full mast. In those days I loved my country madly, and each morning I said "Good day, Chile" to the Andes Mountains. I thought that someday I, too, would put on my best outfit and go to vote with my parents. Then that afternoon it was announced that, by a slim margin, the presidency had been won by Salvador Allende, the doctor who was my father's friend, who brought candy to our house. The eyes of those who had gathered in our living room seemed full of surprise and sadness. Shortly thereafter we had to flee beyond the Andes.

## Pulchritude

He is small, almost diminutive, and ever since I have been aware of him, I knew he was my father. I loved his velvet bathrobes, the orange blossom scent of his shirts. He was a fragrant man, like those we saw accompanying their ladies on seignorial Sundays. But my father smelled of an almost ascetic cleanliness, almost surgical, and to this day, he asks me whether I have been washing my hands and paid my bills. He is interested in my dental hygiene. Now you might imagine that his neatness borders on insanity and obsession, but it is an innocent craziness, almost childlike. It is perhaps the reason why inexplicable things happen to him and only him. For example, he gets toothpaste all over his neckties, jackets, everywhere. Elegant ladies drop quince jam on his pastel shirts. Sick children throw up on his shoes. Of course, he gets mad, yet patiently, as if the world existed in a small bubble of tidiness, he attempts to clean everything up, and enters a zone of muteness. He says nothing, or everything by not speaking. The next day he is once again as clean as always, until it occurs to some desperate person to splat holy water or parsley leaves all over him.

## Tell Me a Story, Papa

"Why don't you tell me a story, Papa?" I asked. "Like the ones Carmen Carrasco tells, fireside stories full of thrills and scary things, stories about ghosts haunting the valleys and the Atacama Desert."

"Tell me a story, Papa," I said. "Something about angels. Omama Helena assures me that Jewish people do have angels, and that they smile like the enlightened birds of this strange, wild country she loves so much."

Then my father slightly sharpened his voice, already too quiet and muzzled. He sat next to me keeping an almost perfect distance, and began: "Once upon a time it was Friday afternoon in the city of Stanislav. Autumn was descending with marvelous fury, the leaves, the wind with its plush noises, the passersby, in love, were preparing for the Sabbath. Haim Halpern, your great-grandfather, was a pious man, a friend to Jews and Christians alike, and he was truly what we call Shomer Sabbath, the keeper of the Sabbath, the man who rests at sunset and communes with God. Haim Halpern had a beautiful building in Stanislav and he sold precious cloth, delicate in texture. His fabrics traveled throughout Europe, from East to West and, it was said, even as far as Fez, where women wore them on high, broad balconies in order to be admired, their bodies swathed in lace and perfumed oils. When Haim Halpern would get ready to go out, your great-grandmother Frida, which means dreams of peace, would wait for him with the clear Sabbath light, fish and braided bread, because she grew in happiness whenever she prepared Shabbat's enchanted potions. Three monks arrived to ask Haim Halpern to sell them some precious fabric for All Saints' Day, and especially to take with them to Jerusalem for Holy Week. Haim Halpern told them that they should wait until Monday because the Sabbath was near, and the lights of Stanislav were blinking. Women walked silently by, it was time for God's evening lights.

"The three monks were quite insistent, and they seemed to have stepped out of a book of illuminations or a Bible," said my father. "Hours passed and the three monks did not relent, but neither did my grandfather because his faith was more dizzying and strong than the three bags of gold that the monks showed him with laconic smiles, more suited to business transactions than to faith. Then they decided to leave the three bags of gold and return on Monday.

"Haim Halpern went home on foot and remembered his father and his father's father, and his father's grandfather, and felt himself falling more deeply in love with Frida, the rhythm of happiness and faith. On Monday he got up very early and prepared to open his shop and await the monks, but they never came, not on Monday nor on Tuesday. Days passed, months, and years, and the religious did not arrive to buy fabric for their Holy Land vestments.

"Haim Halpern called upon the learned man of the city, Rabbi Eliezer Mendele and also wise Frida, who in the farthest reaches of her gaze had guessed the secret of these strange monks. Rabbi Eliezer said that these brothers were angels, God's messengers, trying to test Haim's faith. The money they had left behind was clear proof of the fact that they were not products either imagination or memory, but were indeed messengers of God. Otherwise, how could such an appearance and disappearance be explained? No one knew where they had come from nor where they went, nor by what turbulent road they had vanished, like God's mysterious desert wind.

"Rabbi Eliezer decided it was time for the money to go to Haim, but Haim Halpern was pious and humble, with the subtle elegance of the fortunate. He decided to establish a Hebrew school with that

money he called the Haim Halpern Talmud Schule. This school is
a building razed by the winds of war, but it has survived beyond the
thresholds of history. They say one can still see the doors of the Talmud School. Every Shabbat, very early, when sunlight narrows and
flowers, when the earth gives itself over to the rhythm of bliss, one
can hear the hoofbeat of three invisible horses. And they say, they
are the angels, the three messengers of God."

### *Jewish Dog*

Even the teacher joined in. Ferociously and happily they sang this
song:

> How many loaves in the oven?
> Twenty-one, all burned.
> Who burned them?
> The Jewish Dog.

These were the earliest rhymes, full of ire and hatred, that I heard
in first grade in Santiago de Chile in 1962. The school was four long
blocks from my home, in the old neighborhood of Nuñoa, where
Chilean aristocrats used to stroll along lush avenues shaded by
canopies of oaks and lined with forget-me-nots. After school, my
mother usually picked us up and witnessed our distress. Aware of
our Jewishness, my sister and I regularly cried tears of shame.

The song I have mentioned is still sung today in schools throughout Chile. My mother hears it in Osorno, my father hears it in Quillota, my friend Cristina hears it at the polished British school where
her daughters are enrolled. There is no remorse, no compassion.
On the contrary, when we confronted the teacher, who enjoyed
singing the tune, she felt personally attacked. This is the sad solitude
of my country, the common consciousness. Any sense of responsi-
ble solidarity vanishes like a misty morning along the coast. We hung
our heads as we walked home and in the distance we heard someone
mock us: "There go two Jewish dogs."

My parents decided to send us to an all-Jewish school where no
one would sing that frightful song to us.

## The Hebrew Institute

My school was called the Hebrew Institute of Santiago de Chile, established in the twenties so that the Jewish children of Chile would be spared shouts of "Jewish shit" and questions about their horns. Delighted, my father dropped us off very early each morning so that he could begin to impart molecular laws at 7:40 AM on the far side of town, where students, like sunrise ghosts, learned humble gratitude from sickly neighbors.

The school was secular, with socialist tendencies imparted by the teachers who, for the most part, came from Israel. They spoke to us about free love and the pleasures of touching the soil. They were tall, robust individuals, not at all like the images of tattered Jews seen in the dreadful films about events in Europe that were rarely shown in our part of the world.

The Hebrew Institute was a happy place. Instead of buzzers there were bells, plenty of bougainvilleas and pine trees transplanted from the coast, and energetic rhythms, adolescent and daring. In our Tanaj class we argued with God. In Jewish history class we worried about the Palestinian question long before it became controversial.

We did all this in a school located at 1242 Macul Street. More than anything, we loved our teachers who had to take three or four buses to get to work. The women faculty arrived each morning in scant striped jackets, tinged by frost and poverty. They moved with agility as they approached the blackboards, lit the small portable heaters, and taught us to sing, to read, to be.

Rather than training us to be what in America is called "a functional Jew," our education was wise in the principles of justice and solidarity, in the mysteries of the Kabbala. At that school we did not feel like strangers, we were mischievous children who made fun of Hebrew accents and *gringo* teachers, and regularly stole exquisite milk candies from under Miss Paula's nose in the din of the cafeteria.

## My History Teacher

She was tiny and seemed able to fly in the early morning mist. The wind always scratched her skin. She came to school almost directly from bed, wrapped in a red hand-me-down coat that brought out the smeared red of her lipstick. She always wore a blue beret and woolen gloves that emphasized fingers, bony and sad like a life forsaken or the ache of a broken heart. She was my history teacher, Marta Alvarado, educator at a private school for Jewish girls. She loved incongruous, ambiguous, disorderly, and beautiful history. She didn't care whether we knew the capitals or could draw borders. For her, history was the love between Columbus and Queen Isabella, the grandeur of Eleanor of Acquitaine, the courage of Salome and Ruth.

In Doña Marta Alvarado's history class, women spoke and narrated, they were brave, they wore gloves and sometimes daggers, but never bloody ones. They didn't concern themselves with details, but cherished common sense above all else.

I loved Marta Alvarado. I was her star pupil because she did not require me to recite dates or the false memories of prophets. At her side I read *El Cid Campeador,* and King David, too. She would caress me and kiss me, marking me with the unmistakable imprint of her bright red lips.

The day before we left for America, she arrived in a rumpled taxi, in her red coat and blue beret, with red flowers and pencil. She held in her hands a gift for me. I traveled with that gift, and at night, when I felt like a lost child alone in the city, I invoked Marta Alvarado under another sky and other rain. She was always there, telling me: "Real history was made by women."

## *Hebrew*

From an early age I learned Hebrew, and it seemed like Spanish to me. Each letter is pronounced as it is written. Moreover, each letter is like a small drawing, an animal from beyond the breezes. I liked Hebrew and its legends about harvests and honey, lots of honey. At home I would teach the maids, who barely spoke Spanish, a few words in Hebrew, the holy language, the language of the Chosen, even though I knew God didn't choose anyone, and they were happy with the alphabet of stars.

## Dead Languages

My grandmother used to tell us that she sent us to school in order to learn dead languages and the history of affliction. My father assured us that Hebrew was the key to understanding ways of truth, and I simply liked that school, the Hebrew Institute of Santiago de Chile. The doormen and monitors were all deaf, never batting an eye when students smooched in the hallways, but smiling instead, as if murmuring.

I liked the Hebrew language with its curves, its words that could be fury itself or the most timid and placid of retreats. That language of dead languages was also like things that are loved in secret. At night I used to tell my sister that Hebrew was like invisible fairies, each letter secretly encasing the name of God. To pronounce them was to reach up to that breath, to the memory of faith.

I liked my school. There we were Jews, even at Passover when we played the parts of Egyptians. But we knew we were all slaves and that all our knowledge had first taken shape in Babylonia, Alexandria or Toledo, those capitals of memories.

## The Book of God

The house was surrounded by books. They covered the shelves like reddish manes. My father loved them, and long before I acquired the pleasurable habit of reading, I spent entire afternoons caressing them. I investigated pictures, the musicality of opened pages, the shine of bookmarks. I loved books. I loved them even before I realized that I would find myself in them. Above all, in the deep darkness, when the sky melds into sadness, I took them to the small playroom and created libraries. I secretly kissed the weary words goodnight and sent them off for a well-deserved, melodious rest. My grandfather always had books in German on his night table. He said he brought them from Vienna, that they had crossed the seas, rounded Cape Horn, and that they were his most faithful companions during those days of treacherous crossings. My father was obsessed with collecting books about psychiatry and, in some cases,

the implacable human body. I preferred detailed pictures of flowers, elves, and butterflies. Books ought to look at the invisible, and
the human body seemed all too obvious to me in its simple harmony.

When we left Chile my grandfather gave me his own book, a
greenish logbook, a travel notebook he had titled Paulina after his
first love. In it he jotted notes about youthful love, the Vienna
cabarets, the journeys across the distances and the misty horizons.
This is the book I most adore, and for me it is the book of God.

## Shabbat

My grandfather and I loved Shabbat because they were lethargic yet
fancy days. He used to say that Shabbat creaked like a box full of
tender memories, spruced up and decorated as keepsakes.

There, in the city of Santiago, amid the murmuring Andes Mountains and the warmth of my hand that wandered with him, he recalled his mother placing violets on the table, or crouching on the
paths of Vienna as they kicked her and called, "Juden, Juden." My
grandfather whispers in bed, his body shifting between the sheets,
and I hear him say his mother's and grandmother's names. As the
years go by, the memory becomes ever more distinct, or more sudden. From out of the fog emerges life and the first breaths on God's
still warm lips.

We did all this on Shabbat. We weren't a family to attend ser-
vices at the synagogue, but slowed time down because we wanted
to learn to observe. On Saturdays, my grandfather said, we saw in
double, with both our body and soul. Nothing interrupted us and the
Andean wind blew at our feet like a sweet hurricane. Far in the distance, as the windmills churned in the afternoon darkness, and the
silences were twofold, we would suddenly see an unexpected bright
flame. It was my great-grandmother Helena, waiting for us to receive
our Sabbath queen. The beauty of the street and the lamps blinded
us. That beauty was so lovely and so frightening. We were happy to
return to the house in a land that belonged to no one, but which
was also a land too much our own.

## My Grandfather

My grandfather had enormous green eyes. At times they took on the color of certain rivers, of certain oceans whose rocky waters only he, a solitary sailor, could cross. At other times his eyes seemed like the lush, beautiful forests of Chile. We were much alike, my grandfather and I.

We lied about the walks we took. We said we had crossed the entire city on the back of a white horse, or that we had gone to eat strawberries in the woods. My grandfather had an unbridled imagination, but above all, he had a sense of gratitude, of happiness for life itself. He was a man whose past was filled with grand passions, now left behind in the titillating cabarets of Vienna or the far too dark boardinghouses of Santiago's slums. He liked to give himself certain bits of advice, such as "it costs nothing to be polite," "courtesy, attention to detail, and small gifts are worth a lot," and my favorites: "Why not make your grandmother happy, it costs so little," and "how much money can we save by walking instead of taking a cab?"

My grandfather and I were friends through good times and bad. Sitting in the velvet chair in his elegant lounging jacket, he sometimes thought about the woods of Vienna and those who were unable to escape. I would draw close and attempt to dispel the darkness with a kiss. "Grandfather," I said, "we are in Chile, and tomorrow we will cross the mountains." On Fridays, once the Shabbat light had begun to enter our hearts, my grandfather recited the kaddish, and we prayed for those who no longer could touch the miracle of life, for those who died with shaved heads, for those who never thought they were different, and who had believed in the soul and the human spirit.

## Train Station

In all cities, distant and near, and of all the paths confused by the thickness of time, my grandfather liked the train stations with their puffs of nostalgia and sadness. He watched with curiosity the passengers roaming about, getting off trains, desperate to find that which they had not sought. Sometimes I'd watch him as his eyes became coated with a sense of nostalgia beyond words. It was called sadness, and I came to recognize it later in the faces of other family members. I asked him, "Grandpa, who are you looking for with your desert eyes?" He just took me by the arm, and confused, we returned to the others, for we had become lost in dreams along with the other men and women on the railway platform.

My mother remembers the day she went with José, my grandfather, to the treacherous train station in Osorno, Chile, where women tied their hair with strips of white fabric, sold freshly made candy, and kept the flies at bay. My mother was wearing a suit as blue as her eyes, and she and her father waited to meet the Auschwitz refugees, women who, in the face of life's pain, had become sleepless, solitary and invisible, women who had snuck away.

I always felt that my grandfather's hands were like a single vine, a single wood full of fragrant lilies.

## Aunt Lucha

You've met her. I have mentioned her often, or perhaps you recall her nocturnal hip, floating desperately beyond the balustrades of Viña del Mar. The truth is that my Aunt Lucha, although merciful with the precarious destiny of her own body, did not give equal care to her beloved bones, woven, fragile, and obsolete. Her last surgery was minor. By then, even the term *operating room* made her dilapidated stomach churn, but at last she decided to remove her bunion, which for many years had made her life miserable, yet sometimes pleasant with its small and subtle tickles, saying: "Luchita, this is what happens when you self-medicate. This is what happens when you choose pills according to their color and effects." She and her bunion were like an incompatible married couple, as inseparable as water for chocolate, or the oil and vinegar found on the tables of rich and poor alike, living together but apart.

And so it happened on a warm winter morning, as the rose bushes awoke from their seaside slumber gently bending their petals to greet the old folks rolling by in their chairs, my Aunt Lucha left her house, all dressed up like a shining virgin. That's how she liked to celebrate her surgeries, with green lilies and fuschia lilacs. Her poor husband pushed the wheelchair and carried fruit, onions, and castor oil. He was too good a man, condemned to the sad fate of carrying other people's packages, including those of his beloved Lucha, bedmate, sharer of stories, and sparring partner for more than fifty years.

My Aunt Lucha's operation went without a problem, yet, years later she told us about something strange that had occurred that day. While she was in the hospital, a nun entered her room each evening. She had a white mustache like the late President Allende, and she never knocked. In a hoarse voice, she asked only one question: "Do you want confession?" Softly, my Aunt Lucha always said no. Yet the nun appeared regularly during the entire hospital stay, always at night. My aunt could hear her footsteps approaching, and the beating of wings as of a wounded bat. She never inquired about my aunt's health, only about confession. The final night in that small hospital, where relatives fed the patients chicken soup and friends brought them syringes, the nun came in and asked once more if she wanted confession. Lucha said, "Sister, I am Jewish." Taken aback, the nun rolled about in her sad habit and replied, "How strange. You are far too good to be a Jew."

## Dinner with the Aristocrats

At dinner with members of Chile's aristocracy, hermetic and of ancient lineage, conversation always turned to the Indians, the mestizos, and above all, the greedy, usurious Jews, destroyers of the nation's economy. No one knew my family background, because I was too blond, too refined, too silent. Suddenly I heard someone say, "At next Sunday's barbecue, let's roast a few Jews." Others attributed a somewhat Jewish outlook to an acquaintance, meaning she was greedy, aggressively destructive of men, and lacking in scruples. I looked around the table, then told them I felt a stomachache coming on. The Jewish dog left and went out into the rain and wind.

## The Star of David

I wanted to know what had been said during the war years in southern Chile, in Puerto Montt, Puerto Octay, and the areas surrounded by German settlers who came to those places and loved the thickness of the lakes, the dormant and live volcanoes. My mother lived alongside them, one of the few Jewish girls in her town. Many Nazis fled to Argentina and Chile. They changed their first and last names and took new wives. Some had children but perhaps they retained that absence of pity, so apparent in their gaze, that lack of morality in their souls. I saw them when I strolled through the city with my mother, and when I went to the German League in Santiago de Chile or the German Center in Valdivia. It was 1989, and I asked to see newspapers from 1940 to 1943. They told me with guilty looks that those records had been destroyed in a strange fire. Nothing of the meticulous archives had been saved. Nothing remained of the well-kept history of Chile's southern cone, of those years in which the German presence was considered prestigious, and those who threw lavish parties for Hitler were the most prized of foreigners.

I have a relative who, ashamed of her Jewish heritage, hides the Star of David because the son of Walter Rauf, one of the most notorious Nazis who had fled to Chile, is a business associate of her husband's. He claims that the son had nothing to do with the entire matter, but the father is often a guest in their home. Walter Rauf sits on my cousin's sofa, takes the afternoon tea she prepares, and gives her gifts of exquisite German chocolates. He always brings along a Wagner recording.

Every time Rauf drops by, my cousin hides the Star of David. She cannot bear to look Mr. Rauf in the eye for fear of recognizing the women he murdered at Auschwitz. She would have to celebrate evil, cruelty, and human bestiality.

Mr. Rauf and his son eat and chat about the price of smoked meat. Mysteriously my cousin faints, and as they open her blouse, the blue Star of David, like a mirror of all that is hidden, is revealed. Walter Rauf, accustomed to the sight of stars of David, says he must be going. He acts as if nothing had happened and takes his leave, promising to see them next week at the Union Club.

Walter Rauf and his son live in Chile, home to General Augusto

Pinochet and site of several concentration camps. My cousin's Star of David shines in the perverse darkness of night.

## Thinking about Oblivion

May we not pass into oblivion, my grandmother said, may the existence of Jews be neither nebulous nor silent, and the samovar, the sugar bowl, and the sabbath candles were always present. She tore at her clothing on days of mourning and celebrated the holy seasons with the same food they ate in Russia. There was no assimilation. Rather, the goal was to incorporate the past into the present, to be a Jew in Chile, not a Chilean Jew, because we know that we would be called You, the Jews. We decided to be wise and clever, and to say instead, You, the Chileans.

## A Glorious Body

In a loud, self-assured voice, I repeated to the point of exhaustion, beyond insomnia, that eternal life was to be found on earth, that Paradise was a Sunday full of balloons and trips to the ornate Christian cemeteries, that there was no life beyond this splendid one, and that goodness meant extending a hand, defying anger and hatred and the snares of envy. Then they would get mad, throw stones, and threaten me with hell, where a pile of rocks and two horned Jews stood guard over the entrance to all the austere cemeteries of the world. They did this because they knew not the cadence of flowers, only of rocks.

I grew up without believing in eternal life. I believed in goodness and in this earthly paradise. From our past there were only meager memorials among the ashes. Our future was a winged suitcase ready for any and all flights, and for uncertain returns to places we could not recognize.

One of my dearest friends used to give me cotton candy and tell me that if only I believed in eternal life, my body would return in a state of glory. I imagined myself very, very tall, my hair more golden than Marilyn Monroe's, and my legs as sinuous as a mermaid's fin.

Only then, in the brief vastness of a second, did the idea of eternal life appeal to me. Only then did I want to be a Christian, so I could return to this earthly paradise as a glorious body.

## They Say

My friend Doris is not allowed to play with me because I am Jewish. Her mother says that Jews are strange. They grow horns at night, they don't eat pork, they chase children, and they like to bathe in Christ's blood. I listen, and her fable thrills me. Still, I don't believe Jews are a bloodthirsty people, and I tell her so. She pats me on the head, which is round and silky. No horns yet.

My great-grandmother says that the Germans were like no other people she had ever encountered. She felt them arrive at dawn, slip into the garden, that beloved garden full of violets, poppies, and errant birds. She said they seemed like large angels dressed in black.

My nana says that one shouldn't speak to Gypsies because they don't bathe and they like to boil children in lizard soup.

My neighbor goes to the nuns' school, and she says that when you secretly touch yourself at night, the devil comes to get you, and he sucks all the blood from your private parts.

They told me all this, and more.

## Confessions

She used to tell me that I was too beautiful and kind to be a Jew, that my almost albino complexion hid my Semitic features. I told her that during one of the pogroms, while my great-grandparents' house burned to the ground, a member of my family must have been raped, and that is why my face and soul were different from all the rest. She told me to go with her to see the confessor. Restlessly she sang the Our Father off-key and murmured prayers like frightening lamentations.

She said she had stolen other people's desires and robbed the happiness of others. She called herself perversely astute. The priest listened to her and took delight in her small pleasures. I was seated further back, my legs crossed, thinking about my genitals, my shoes full of astonished holes and colored stones. I didn't like this act of confession, a ritual lacking water, sense, and mirrors. The shadows surrounding it were much too dark.

She later emerged, sovereign and in control, and told me all her crimes had been absolved. She asked me about my sins and about eternal life in the other world. I told her I loved this world, that our planet seemed seductively beautiful, with its rules and secret prophecies, like dreams of violet candlesticks. This is Paradise, I told her, and God is in our offerings, in a breeze full of small enchantments. Paradise is counting the trees and the stars. Her expression became cloudy, and she asked, "Wouldn't you like to be resurrected in a glorious body?" I told her I'd settle for a body like Marilyn Monroe's, but only here, on earth.

## The Godmothers

The luckiest girls had godparents. They spoke of their godmothers as of fairies, visitors wrapped in violet-colored mist and hair. The godmothers carried colored baskets full of herbs for good luck, especially in love, and unusual flowers from forest groves.

I did not have a godmother, nor would I have a First Communion nor a Bat Mitzvah; only boys had Bar Mitzvahs. They had all the privileges, from the most sumptuous seats in the synagogue to the best piece of chicken at Passover. We girls were given the skinniest slices. We sat in the back of the synagogue, lacking godmothers. No women with rice-powdered faces arrived to stroke our hair.

The destiny of a Jewish girl was to look at photograph albums full of dead aunts incinerated at Auschwitz or Dachau. Those women were her godmothers. I kept watch, but there were no graves on which to place bouquets of violet-colored flowers for them. The guardians of my dreams are my dead godmothers.

## Photographs I

Every afternoon, when sunlight plowed the sky during the hour of reposed meditation, when the adults played abundant games of love in dark rooms, and when sinuous time became ambiguous, I would go with the servants to a room that smelled smoky, violet, a darkish room with curtains that retained the innocent smell of things no longer wanted by anyone.

I would go to that room and lean into photographs that had nothing to do with war or forgetting. They were photographs that marked the able passing of fertile time, commemorations of births and First Communions, young loves, taken in some now hazy provincial plaza. The photographs belonged to the maids, whom I never considered our servants, the women who protected me from the sea of love and the sniffles. Those women were the true keepers of time and memory, cherished like a picture of God on a holy card, because they didn't know how to read or write. So they remembered time through images that always accompanied them, indicating the correct path in life and the ire of death. Perhaps those photographs were the guardian angels of my childhood, in harmony with the photos of horror placed in the most remote nooks of my house: the photo of my cousin calcined in Auschwitz, the photo of my Uncle Mauricio on the Hamburg docks before being deported to the incurable camps of damned barbed wire. I grew up with those photos, but also with those in the maids' quarters, celebrations of death. The deceased were there, on the wobbly night table, surrounded by candles, forget-me-nots, and sighs, like the always smiling face of God. And the maids, naive, spoke to those photos, those lost provincial postcards. When the women spoke of death, they rocked back and forth and laughed, plucking the petals from mischievous flowers gathered in the fields during the day, then placed just so on the table, next to the winking image celebrating that strange past of poverty and happy moments. The photographs were never silent, they were changeable, smiling. At times my mother said I smelled like a poor person because I spent so much time with the maids. But I really smelled of happiness because I didn't have to think about what had happened to Aunt Eduvigis or to the little boy dressed like an angel. They had all died of natural causes, of indigestion or sorrow. No one had shaved their heads and put them on those saddest of trains, golden trains lost in countries of smoke. Sometimes, when I cry, I imagine certain photographs in the maids' rooms. They are not distant photographs, they are very beautiful. I can't make out whether they laugh or cry, whether they fade in the light and shadow, but I know that they are celebratory, that it is possible to sing in their presence or to reinvent scenes of love.

I like these photographs. They are like a gust of fresh spring water, they are the holy water that the women bring home from church and sprinkle between their legs. They have nothing to do with the certainty of death, nor of loss or absence. There they are, full of lilies, and they spin and linger like a caress.

## Photographs II

There were the photographs, laid out on a small table in the living room, neither hidden nor present. These were photographs of distant relatives, aunts from Vienna, cousins from Poland, great-grandparents from Odessa, but most of all, they were photographs in soft sepia, the color of love. I liked to linger over them and peer intently at them because I felt that in those faces there was a voice like a bridge leading to the secret of dreams. My aunts dressed in black and wore tulle hats. Something in their expressions recalled the faces of witches, magicians, fairy godmothers come from strange lands. They fluctuated in the photographs, which were full of silences and nocturnal birds.

Almost all the photographs had been taken in a garden or in the Vienna woods. They were serene, calm. Life seemed peaceful and rhythmic like a river, full of fruit trees and distracted silences. My aunts smiled. My younger female cousins winked. It was around 1938. I liked to greet them each morning, to brush my hair that seemed so much like theirs. I also liked to name them, because I had a similar name, and by saying it, I was able to find myself.

Nothing remains of those women. Some died in the chambers of blue gas, others disappeared in those cities that once had been lovely, cities that once knew how to caress their footsteps. Where are those gardens tended by my ancestors? Who took care of the gardenias, the violets, the rickety rubber plant in the foyer? I looked at those photographs every morning of my childhood. I liked the settings that reflected the shadow of particular gazes, worlds beyond memory and history. I like to gaze at a destiny unfulfilled and invent a future, because the women in the photographs never had a chance to be. They died in gardens of ashes where I return in dreams to visit them.

These photographs survived the time of ire, of perverse madness, when it was not possible to save anything because bodies had to flee quickly, as if struck by a whip or by lightning. One had to leave shawls and coats behind, take nothing and obey orders. Somehow these photographs were all that was rescued, the refuse of history and its ashes. My grandmother used to look at them every morning and sometimes took her leave of them at night when her lamentations turned to prayers or thin supplications. I knew that I couldn't ask her anything because no one was sure what had happened to Cousin Emma or Aunt Eva. No one could tell me anything about the photographs, the day they were taken on a stroll through the woods of Vienna, along the shore near Hamburg. At times the photographs denounce what lies behind the serenity of their images. As I looked at those photographs, I saw only death, like a pack of hounds with blue horses, bodies quivering with fear, fleeing their houses, streets, cities, brutally condemned to board the death trains. That's what the photographs tell me about those who no longer exist. That's why no one speaks of them, because they are gone, like the night and its fugitives. That image of history became the stuff of my dreams, the stupor of my pain. I saw my aunts and cousins in modest, serene gardens, every flower in place. But beyond time came throats of smoke, broken strands of hair and the garden became a single flame of broken glass, of mist, of oblivion. Nothing remained from that time of the families who strolled or conversed in that garden. Nothing remained. All that existed was a scorched silence like a changeable photograph, submerged in desertion. My life, like my history, had been cut short with them. My voice is a mooring line beyond the silences.

## Photographs III

My recollection, my memory, existed through them, the photographs that my mother caressed and visited every afternoon, like ritualistic lovemaking in the shadows. I spied on her the way young girls spy on mothers they adore. In the afternoon she would take the photographs out of their darkened coffers and draw near to them. She seemed to choose that hour for its mistiness, the confusion of light and shadow. It was the time of day when ghosts emerge from captivity.

My mother contemplated the photograph of my grandfather cleaning the gravesite of his own father in Vienna. There were other photos of women suspended in time, in the evanescent night. She used to say, "Perhaps this is the last picture taken of her. This is the last time she went into her garden to breathe the fresh, moist air, the last time she felt her soft wool shawl on the curve of her shoulders."

My mother played in a vanished world of things and objects lost in time. My mother had the good sense to talk to her photographs often, to visit them, dance with them, and bind them to her intrepid heart.

# Chapter Three

# The Women

## The Jewelry

On bold, rainy days in Santiago, when school was a distant fragrance, I liked to be sick until four in the afternoon. My mother wisely sensed that whatever I did not learn in the classroom that particular day, I would master later on in the inescapable apprenticeship of life. That's how the tradition of lending me her jewels began.

She kept them in a small, sky blue suitcase the color of air. The jewelry wore the memory of that first trip to Buenos Aires when my grandmother strolled between Palermo and the Plaza de Mayo with my grandfather José. The case contained the jewelry of my dead aunts, who somewhere in God's world lie seared between what is forgotten and what is unloved.

According to my mother, the jewelry case had been brought from Prague. Covered with small garnets, it seemed both fragile and strong, suspended in the illusion of an ocean crossing. What did my great-grandmothers keep in the box? Everyday costume jewelry or earring and pendants worn to fashionable evening parties? The jewelry box was a peaceful guardian of a Europe that no longer existed, of a time and place that was now a series of small, nameless urns buried in mountains of ash and gardens replete with bones.

And still the jewelry box made me happy. Rescued from oblivion, it contained rings that had belonged to my cousins from Vienna and my great-grandmother Helena's sepia-colored pendants. I imagined those bracelets, the solitary and pained tiaras, stretched out in the dry air, with no one to keep track of their steps, their stories. That's what war jewelry is like, immobile, detained, without generations or the longevity of love. I liked the jewelry because it was like strings connected through time to another's memory. I played with the various pieces, I caressed them so they would shine, so they would be very near to the breath of God, and therefore be able to live.

## Looking-Glass Memory

I grew up imagining and reinventing the woods and parks of Vienna. My great-grandmother Helena repeated the names of the flowers she used to buy on Sundays at the corner stand, and would thank the toothless Chilean vendor in German. On Friday evenings, when the mountains of the Andes with their transparent, whitish frosting descended upon the city of Santiago, my great-grandmother lit candles like beacons of love at the end of the earth. She prayed silently, then spoke to us of the streets of her childhood, of her mother's photographs, of evening walks when the Prater was yet a wood abloom in lilies. Was it possible for her to remember the city, those countries lost in hatred, and still face the world wearing an expression of hope, wrapped in a chrysalis of love? All my great-grandmother ever did was remember, and I remembered along with her, because to forget meant quite simply to die, or worse, that she never lived in Vienna, perhaps not even in Europe. Were she to return to that city now, were I to return, she wouldn't be able to show me the corner where she used to buy flowers. My great-grandmother came from a decimated universe. To make it real, she had to invent it, reconstruct it, weave strands of tangled memories that weren't really true either.

Perhaps for my great-grandmother, for Jews in general, remembering is a way of rescuing the past. It also means a permanent state of mourning for what was or never was, for the calcined wardrobes, for the face of fear in unlived childhoods. I understood this very quickly and felt that being Jewish had to do with what was hopelessly lost. At times I saw my great-grandmother studying strange maps of old towns. She repeated their names, shaking her head. The towns that had once shared her destiny no longer existed. What could Santiago de Chile offer Helena Broder? One day I asked her, "What has become of you, really?" And she told me, without being surprised, that she was an absence, a vanishing body.

My entire family has been part of these far-flung, intermittent exiles, as if life were a journey on a ship of fools, with no hope of return. Along the way we held on to what is fleeting, but also to life itself, because my memory became accustomed, in Vienna, in Prague, to feather pillows, jams, burnt books, and the need to reinvent oneself.

## Helena of Vienna

My great-grandmother loved white doves, writing implements in antique pencil holders perched on the edge of each and every abyss. But most of all she loved sugar. Sugar with stiff lemon slices in herbal tea, sugar on sandwiches, sugar on strawberries and French cheese. She said it was from Sonia, her own mother, that she inherited her love of sweetness, her love of that bejeweled powder, light and transparent. Sugar sweetened the sadness of those who had been displaced, soothed their hunger and made their crossings sweeter, less painful and solitary. Sugar was like life without the clouds.

My great-grandmother Helena used to sit happily for hours looking at rings with keys to the house in Vienna. She kept them in her debris-filled trunk. She also spent lots of time deciding on just the right place for her many lost items, knowing full well that no one knew, and never would know where they were. Sometimes my great-grandmother would take sheets of paper and shoot them into the wind. She said they were messengers from secret places. I asked her about the possessions she had left behind in the lost streets, and she told me that she was unbent by the past, that this was not a time for lamentations, and that those padlocks would open other doors, other windows.

My great-grandmother's gaze was filled with solitude and separateness. She carried many silences to and from foreign ports, her dark shoes, the only witnesses to the sinister time. She was an old-fashioned lady, like those that are found on holy cards of Virgins, her hair and gaze the color of silver. She spent hours pouring over maps of sunken cities, territories where man had crashed in the abyss of his own cruelty.

My great-grandmother was from Vienna. Nothing remains of her house filled with books, her hazelnut-scented garden, only the debris and the desolation of that afternoon when they came in search of her, demanding the keys to that house in her beloved city. I never learned more details of my great-grandmother's life in Vienna. She never spoke to me about her belongings or their abandonment. She never recalled out loud the names of her dead friends. She never spoke of infernal Europe and of that abrupt time that condemned her to an exile devoid of memory.

My great-grandmother walked slowly. She seemed distracted amid days and nights, but when she prepared the Sabbath, she glowed with joy, dressed in lace, and told me, "Dear Granddaughter, the most important thing is to believe in angels." Before lighting the Shabbat candles, my great-grandmother Helena said that we should imagine ourselves in what was called the ends of Sacred Eternity. She then produced two Viennese candlesticks, which she had managed to save, and sighed as she returned deeply to the past. She covered her head with a silver veil that framed her misty hair. My great-grandmother prayed.

We are in the southern part of the world. The passing birds look with curiosity at candles lit in the afternoon, and my grandmother prays for the homes abandoned, for the vestiges of what once lived and possessed memory. I accompany her in her chores and in her murmurs to a strange and at times insensitive God. Although my father has told me that God does not exist, I pray, and my prayers calm my spirit, the landslides, the nearby wars. My great-grandmother prays for Shabbat, for Sundays, and for all Jews and Christians expelled from God's paradise.

## A Book of Faces

At her round table my great-grandmother Helena cuts bits of paper into shapes of moons and muzzled fairies. The ladies of the neighborhood hurry to bring her well-traveled and ancient magazines, and she cuts out dislocated figures with her porcelain hands. She spends hours bent over a three-legged table cutting out shapes. At times she howls as if naming certain cities of fire and stone. Sometimes she strips the paper shapes and says they are the lilies of the Prater or the woods of Vienna. At the age of eight I sit beside her for this early morning ritual, cutting out paper figures and placing them in a sepia-colored album, wrinkled like a quivering tree, like threads of sun amid gusts of wind. She gives each figure a name, cups them in her hands, then blesses them as they enter the great book of life.

It was a most beautiful book of immortal faces. Twenty years later I visited women in Buenos Aires who cut out the photographed faces of their dead children. I visited El Salvador and there they told me that the wind of absence blows on the broken faces of the dead, just as my great-grandmother and I used to blow on the ancient cutouts, reconstructing the lives of people we never met. Not just lives, but thousands of cities, thousands of lost stars, and children's shoes in mountains of smoke.

## Autumn

My great-grandmother Helena liked to walk in search of autumn because she said she thought she could hear the sea over deserts filled with leaves. Very late in the afternoon, when the hour of silence is transparent and the air, in flight, languishes in peace, my great-grandmother Helena would gaze at the sky and recognize certain points of light, stars. Then, and only then, did she light the Sabbath candles, blessing her dead sisters and her living grandchildren. She prayed that the Chileans would treat the Indians with mercy. I watched her, alone in the immense room, and the candelabras seemed like small, fragile eyelids whose orbs had witnessed the crossing, mad pilgrimages in search of refuge. The Viennese candelabras were the only survivors of that cruel era in which humankind forgot how to have mercy.

My great-grandmother lit the candles. Bent into the light, her hair whitened before the flame. On just such a Saturday afternoon she gave me a copy of *The Diary of Ann Frank*, and I cut the photographs from it and put them near my bed, on the nightstand, where they remain today. Frau Helena, too, kept a photograph in the same place, a picture of my great-grandfather Isidoro Broder, who disappeared in Vienna in 1932.

When I read the diary I, too, died, my head shaven, my arms tattooed. I decided to wear long sleeves from then on to hide my lacerated skin. My hope, my naked, unworried innocence ended forever with the reading of the diary of Anne Frank because I stopped believing in human goodness and unselfish acts. I also thought that Anne and I could have been friends. We were loners, strangers in imagined and imaginary countries. We could have written together about matters of love.

Then I understood the solemnity of Friday nights at my great-grandmother Helena's house. She didn't need anyone's company when she prayed, it was more a matter of a solitary murmuring, as if her voice were an island surrounded by voices known only to her. It was as if her gaze traversed lost prairies where women dreamed about a light from beyond the heavens.

On those Friday nights, spent at Helena's side, I learned to listen to the wind, to the high heels of women in flight, to screams, and doors that slam, and worm-eaten hearts. All this I learned while Frau Helena prayed as if the night were deep and wide, as if the night had an immense lap, and the sound of trains made her body tremble like candles, like golden autumn light.

## Omama Helena

And my hand traces the features of her face, or could it be wakeful memory tracing time outside of time? I approach you, Omama Helena, your distant and other face between the dark area that frames your visage and its shadows. You are as absent, but it is you there in the Vienna house, on a street that does not exist, in a plaza that only I gropingly traverse, because blindness soothes the disturbances of the soul.

Helena, my great-grandmother, portion of my memories and name of all my names, I approach you on tippy toes and repeat that

I do not know anything about the country you left behind, your rambling search for strawberries and bread.

Great-grandmother, caress of all my encounters, familiar and desired skin, today you appear in the wonder of the ebb and flow of the seasons, when the breeze, the rain, and the bridges of orange blossoms burst forth and shine. You are there, clutching two of your children to your breast, foreseeing every threat.

Great-grandmother Helena with an *H*, Viennese lady, I approach your face and the dialogue with all the dead, with a tapestry of relatives never before seen, like the signals of stars above your hair. The photograph is mute, and the night's heart was dark when you, my Helena, dressed in sequins, fled terrified into the Viennese night, off to a country of strangers, to town squares where friends no longer recognized you.

## A Bit of Luck

Above all my memory recalls that voice, a very deep voice, as if born of the depths of fire, the voice of my grandmother who sang after kissing us goodnight, invoking guardian angels, invisible souls without names, and the Virgin Mary.

My great-grandmother Sonia sang to us in Yiddish and her voice seemed like sadness lost in snow. Her song asked life to grant us a bit of luck, just a tiny little bit of luck. With that voice she put us to sleep amid the trouble and confusion of wartime, amid memories of the dead huddled in trenches. Despite all of this her voice was soft, and it drew sweet applause from our eyelids at rest.

## Grandmother's Shoes

My grandmother Raquel, the cigarette smoker from Odessa, said she loved shoes because in them she returned to the amber coasts of the Baltic Sea. She said that shoes full of stories, full of restless and inquisitive eyes, enabled her to open a path through the excess, beyond the brambles and the restless bouts of insomnia.

My grandmother collected shoes under a high bed made of ivory-colored wood. Throughout the province and the city of Quillota, the city of churches and avocado plants, she was known for her collection of astonishing shoes. People said she named them, talked to them in hushed tones before going out, said good morning to them. She went dancing in her new shoes, my grandmother from Odessa. She had left the Black Sea coast shoeless, but her feet turned amber in color, full of nights and dawns.

## Chepi

Her real name was Hanna. The Chilean border official did not know what to make of that silent Hebrew *H*, so he renamed her Josefina, and her nickname became Chepi. I loved Grandma Chepi above all others, and she admitted she was crazy about me. She was brilliant, according to her brothers and sisters, for she never worked a day in her life. She didn't even know how to boil water for tea. She allowed herself to be loved and caressed, and in return she gave us goodness and justice. She was wise in her pronouncements and chose to lead a bold life. She refused to learn to the art of cooking, or the endless ways to clean a house. She resisted ordering the servants about, and made up her mind to go deaf.

In effect, my grandmother decided not to hear, and she took refuge in her own voice, speaking aloud on topics of her own choice. She rejected hearing aids and medications. When she could no longer see, she cleaned her eyeglasses, and little by little, people began to leave her alone, at peace, as she hoped. She lead a haphazard and precise life. Since she never ate dinner during daylight hours (only chickens and other bad-smelling creatures did so), she always delighted in the sunset over the Pacific Ocean. She was very exact about all four of her daily meals, and allowed no one to forget the sacredness of tea time. There was nothing British about her, quite the contrary. Josefina said she loved Chile and wouldn't trade it for anything in the world, because Chile was the last spot on earth where she could lose herself and be happy. As someone from Chile she need not worry about her family tree or her ancestors. She says, What use is there in speaking Yiddish, the language of suffering, or in beating one's breast, or in praying to an obstinate God? My grandmother says all this smiling broadly and eating ham on holy days.

My grandmother and I have always been crazy about each other. I like to watch her at night as she approaches my bed, and to smell her scent of lavender or alcohol. At times she asks if my husband gives me his permission to travel alone, or if I am in love. She listens, no matter what I say in reply. Sometimes I lie to her, sometimes I tell her the truth.

When I was a child she gave me sweet things, jams. She confessed she was not fond of children or animals in general, but that she loved me. And that's how I grew up, adored by her, wrapped in her luxuriant shawls, in love with all her stories. Now I pay her surprise visits. She is absorbed in Viennese waltzes, she recalls all the trips she never wanted to take and that are now her only light, her altar and her memory. Suddenly, I know that she is my guardian angel because she predicts dangers that lie in my path, advises me to take care of my body, and her face appears to me during hellish nights and in sweet dreams.

Of all deaths, I fear hers the most because she is my memory, and if she ceases to exist I might not know whom to kiss, nor how to distinguish gestures of love and peace. But she is still alive and I think about her. It's like drawing close to the brightness of the sun, to enchanted insects, to good-luck lizards. That is my grandmother, subversive and insistent, a native of Buenos Aires but fervently Chilean, inhabitant of Valparaíso, knitter of enormous scarves, inducer of sleep, and enemy—-like me—of eggplant.

## Travelers

All my grandmothers were travelers. None crossed the Atlantic on luxury liners, but rather in small, fragile boats that defied the sea and its spells. My grandmother Josefina chose a journey over land, across the Andes Mountains by mule. Others chose the fierce, silvery ocean. They arrived in a country that might as well have been landlocked, a city in the desert. It could have been the highlands of Bolivia, but the saltwater forest of Chile's landscape accommodated broken Europe.

Josefina arrived in Chile by mule, and she was the one least affected by the trauma of exile. In truth, she didn't believe in the Diaspora, and knew that the only possible place life could go on was at the end of the earth, in Chile. My grandmother never complained about her luck. She was not interested in stirring genealogical ashes. Her concern was always for the art of living, the happiness of leisure, a well-served cup of tea. Although she is not wealthy, nor an heiress, she has never worked a single day for anyone. A host of servants surround her, fan her in moments of stupor, peel and section her oranges, and cut delicate bits of gristle from her meat.

My grandmother was the daughter of immigrants, as were all my relatives. The suitcases strewn around the house resonated loudly. The words Diaspora, exile, refugee featured prominently in my childhood lexicon. Yet my grandmother always said she was from Chile, a marvelous country she would never leave.

## The Deaf

Little by little my grandparents, aunts, and uncles lost their hearing. They required some words, but not others, to be repeated. They were selective about what they should or did not want to hear, but dangerously aware of certain sounds and words. My grandmother, for example, perked up her ears every time debts were mentioned, her own or those of others. She demanded perfect silence when anyone spoke about the many crooks that had taken advantage of the family since our arrival in Chile aboard mules and third-class trains. On the other hand, my Aunt Eduvigis heard only her squabbling siblings, who usually fought over demijohns of wine or the beauty of their granddaughters. In these instances they perceived every word uttered by the other perfectly. I became accustomed to all their deafness. I read mercilessly erotic love poems aloud, and they didn't listen to me. Sometimes I'd come home at midnight, say hello, then leave for a party, slamming the massive front door of the dilapidated family mansion on my way out. I'd return the following midnight and repeat the entire routine, slam and all, without anyone taking the least notice of me.

Living with deaf people has its charms, such as playing the piano whenever one likes. Deafness offers a wonderful independence, by which certain sounds are put into relief. One can even buy a trumpet and revert to childhood. Above all, deafness creates possibilities, and allows one to hear only what one wishes, to select the fragile and delicious bit of gossip, to sharpen one's ear whenever great secrets are discussed, and all the while remain very close to the silence of God.

## My Aunts

My aunts get together to chat everyday at noon. This is their ritual of love, of sorority in old age, and they keep their midday appointment with zeal, convening at the same place, at the corner shaped by gentle gusts of wind. Coffee with cream at five past twelve. Those who arrive at ten past take their usual places and say hello. The conversation is pleasant, light: the price of coffee, of shoes, and of those tiny southern fruits called wild strawberries, but my aunts always return, hearts bleeding, to the realm of that first crossing, where my grandmother tells the story of her journey, crossing the Andes on a mule, and how the Chileans changed her name to Josefina although her real name is Hanna. Suddenly another of the women takes up the timely chorus of recollection, and asks if anyone remembers Cousin Adelina who, when she arrived from Sebastopol, didn't know what gift to get for the family, so she gave us a chest of drawers that was held up in customs for more than a year. Another aunt says obviously Adelina didn't think we had chests of drawers in Chile. A third aunt, the one with the most distant voice, like a lost echo, asks if anyone remembers the Deresunskys, whose real name was Drullinsky, but they kept Deresunsky because they preferred the later "u" sound.

They part with a "God willing," as Christians say. Raquel promises they will see one another soon. They return to widowhood and its perfidious absence, go home to prepare more stories for the following day's coffee. They are alive.

## Tamara

Tamara was her name and her gaze was like a river, a deep well. She was like a lost soul. Sometimes she looked at us, and was luminous. At times her scarred face emitted nothing but one long complaint for days on end. Tamara Broder came from Prague and was married to Josef Broder, my Viennese grandfather's first cousin. On Shabbath she and her husband came to our house to spend the day, drink afternoon tea, and speak German.

Tamara was translucent and fearless. They say that as they transferred her to a camp in darkened Europe, she fell off the truck. Assuming she was dead, they left her on the side of the road. But it was not yet her time to perish. Tamara survived, only to learn that she no longer had a mother or father, brothers or cousins. Her past had disappeared on that truck headed for the gas chambers.

When I was a child I did not understand Tamara Broder in her dark dresses. Tamara without cousins, Tamara alone beyond the gardens, sobbing.

## Small Change

At times I contemplated them as if lost. Who were these thin, taciturn women in red skirts? Who were the women who arrived as strangers at our home? They came from afar, smelling of foreign places, of poverty marked by coal and wheat, they smelled like poor people.

Many of them traveled to the capital with enormous straw baskets in which they carried their meager belongings. Suddenly, like emaciated fairies, they inhabited our houses, and knew where lost objects hid, where each thing could be found. My mother was always tolerant and noble with the strangers who year after year came to live with us, sharing the footsteps of each and every rumor. Some appeared by means of articles clipped from the Jewish Federation newspaper, because they themselves preferred to work for a Jewish family. I wanted to imitate their charms, their curses, their nighttime games, their fears for children born in backrooms.

I learned all this from them, and from my mother I learned not to ask for the change when they returned from the market. This is a concession one makes to the poor. Never ask them to account for money that has been freely given, as it is our only form of generosity. This I have learned, and to this day I don't ask anyone to account for each penny, not even myself.

## My Cousin Rafael

When the light poured out something akin to soft mist, my elderly uncle and aunt, fasting by the darkness and branches of tenuous light, spoke of old memories. I heard them discuss Cousin Rafael, son of Uncle Jaime from San Felipe and nephew of Uncle Moisés from Buenos Aires. Rafael himself was from nowhere. Exile and atavistic poverty had dogged his steps. Among other things, he was a soccer player, a cabaret pianist, a cardiologist, and a poet. Ever since I was a small girl I liked to hear and say his name, wrapping my tongue around the letter *l*. My cousin Rafael, I heard, fell in love with my mother when they were teenagers. He loved her violet eyes and firefly voice. But since in those days he played the violin in darkened neighborhoods and was not yet either a soccer player or a medical student, he could not compete for the hand of sweet Frida of Osorno.

Years passed, the days grew fat. Rafael's words and stories about him shifted within the incongruous forgetfulness of senility. Still Rafael continued not to be from San Felipe nor the Bellavista neighborhood. He was a son of the San Felipe branch of the family, the Drullinskys, not Deresunskys, even though they really were one and the same. With time he became Cousin Rafael from New York, and he owned a home in the city of a thousand languages, multicolored stores and matching sets of beads.

I stopped being concerned. Cousin Rafael had found his place in the world, and people stopped speaking about him except very distantly every New Year's Eve. They said, "Oh, yes, but do you remember how Rafael played the violin? Better than anyone. And his eyes rolled up and down as if he were touching the sky."

One day my grandmother wrote, in one of her rigorous, weekly letters, that Rafael had finally arrived. He was no longer from New York, no longer either a banker or a violinist. He was now a poet, dazzling me further.

My cousin Rafael had the delicate walk of a sweet man. He was a beautiful gentleman struggling between what was modern and the gestures of the past. One day my great-aunt, who was really my grandmother Drullinsky's or Deresunsky's first cousin, heard the mad music return to Viña's sunny shores. We knew then that true love had been rekindled between Rafael and his childhood sweetheart Astrid, whom my aunts and uncles called Ingrid because they couldn't remember Astrid. Now Rafael is no longer from New York. He is the cousin who used to live in New York. For me, Cousin Rafael is the angel who came back to this city to take care of all those tricky aunts and uncles, to keep them company as they stroll through the sunlit plazas and dream of their daily cup of coffee, lines of poetry and love. Rafael listens to them, harmonizes their cadences, and above all, loves my grandmother Josefina, daughter of Chofi from Buenos Aires. Rafael is not from San Felipe nor Viña. He is an angel who arrived to take care of his elders.

## You'll Learn It Tomorrow

My grandmother wasn't concerned about homework, nor whether we cleaned out our pockets. Chaos, papers smeared with apricot, broken kites, and stones, these were the essential elements of an education. She was hardly solemn about authority, and that's why instead of fasting on certain holy days, we hid behind doors and nibbled slices of ham, winking once at her devout husband and again at God. My grandmother believed that children should spend time outdoors, in the sun, and lots of time playing in bed with fake old-fashioned treasures, costume jewelry and porcelain dolls, old photographs of dead family members, in order to get to know our ancestors. The most marvelous thing about my grandmother was that when we didn't want to go to school, and we asked to stay home, playing in bed with beads and the music of well-traveled harps, she would immediately say yes, and tell my mother, "Frida, what they don't learn today they will learn tomorrow."

Sometimes we simply didn't go to school. We took a break from the tedium of mathematics and correct penmanship. We played, we unstrung beads, and we laughed. My mother began to follow her mother's lead, and when we first moved to Berkeley, California, where the springtime sun is a bundle of corn-colored braids, I asked my mother to take me to pick yellow flowers in the fields. She replied: "Okay, what you don't learn today, you will learn tomorrow." That's how it was. She powdered my face with her compact puff so that later on my teacher would find me pale and weak, and we would leave as if headed to a victory party. We lunched with the flowers, the birds, the wild and beautiful wind. There are many things that I put off until tomorrow, and in so doing, I was perhaps able to learn what really matters: wisdom, ambiguity, irreverence, happiness, ignorance, faith, how to enjoy a day full of amber and accept the invitation of a giddy sea. The rest we learn tomorrow or never because the future is nothing more than the present: the essence of a field full of mint or a journey across transparency.

## Superstitions

My mother wasn't superstitious, but she loved fortune-tellers and their omens, weightless as dragonfly wings. She liked to imitate the gestures of amateur practitioners of the esoteric and the perversely occult. Of all her superstitions I recall with happiness this one: When you speak of the dead, and happen to sneeze, you must give your ears a tug.

## To Breathe

Once my mother told me to breathe deeply, like that, very deeply, as if touching the sea, air, and wind. She made me close my eyes and hold out my hands, palms up, like someone clearly receiving an offering. She gave me small and fragrant stones, fresh from the immense seaweed-filled depths. She also gave me the feathers of lost birds and some sand that moved and played. The day was marvelous, completely clear and cloudless. She said to me, "Here you have the universe in your hands and at your feet. You will not walk this earth as a stranger."

## Chapter Four

# The Guardians of childhood

*Happiness*

I followed my nana because I liked how she knelt to collect dust, re-fining it in the gathers of her skirt, as if it were a precious com-modity. Perhaps she knew the secrets of the crockery and all the pitchers because her mother was an ancient potter. I wanted her to tell me the secrets of the wet clay while she rubbed perfume into the loam, whose fragrance could be detected only in the afternoons. She told me that the secret, just like happiness, was revealed only at the moment of certain cadences, in the pitch of the weft, in the out-lines. She was indeed happy from the moment the sun began to rise and greet the world.

My mother simply greets the morning. She says, "Good morn-ing, Chile!" I pronounce this same greeting in all the borrowed ter-ritories and foreign places. I rest on that greeting as if I had arrived at my true destiny, the most sublime ship.

But what was happiness? In what corner did it hide? It wasn't enough to hold an open hand stretched out or to never allow the southern winds nor the sun to perch on your skin. What was hap-piness? Was it perhaps the flow of uncertain time, beyond the sea-sons, the flow of tanned skin, maker of work and prophecies?

My nana looked at me through copper eyes that approached the indefinite time of moss. Then she told me that happiness was something like fireflies.

## The Servants

As night drew near to bodies craving rest and permanence between the starched, white sheets, the household servants returned to their rooms, traversing the dark kitchen, its shadows made greasy by the fried midnight meal. They slid as if invisible to the backrooms. From an early age I loved to accompany them and hear soap operas on the radio, especially those in which a poor girl finds happiness in the fragile love of a wealthy young man. I liked the nanas because in them I witnessed something close to the truth. Their words were like a light drowsiness, they lacked false modulations. I liked to hear them sing Mexican music here in the southern hemisphere. I liked to wrap myself in their clothing, and to feel the delicious caress of their hands roughened by dead fish and flour.

In the maids' quarters there was a freestanding wardrobe without doors. Instead, an old curtain covered its opening, like a blue canvas on which flies, small reptiles, and bees lit up in the summertime. There wasn't much in the wardrobe: a pleated Sunday skirt in a plastic bag, polished black shoes. The servants' poverty was light, simple, ready to pack up at a moment's notice, perhaps rush off to the north or the south, always living in rooms owned by others, always being what their employers termed a necessary evil.

At night in the maids' quarters we sat in the most sordid yet marvelous darkness. They told me their stories through a collection of photographs, delicate and misty images taken in plazas in the late afternoon. These images, not alphabets, brought order into their past. There were many pictures of other women's children, youngsters for whom the servants had cared rigorously, loving them, dressing them, white children whose bodies they had smelled. The servants' lives were equally enmeshed with those of the well-to-do young matrons who hired backroom maids to bathe their children so that they could sip wine at midnight, aloof, alone, and free.

During my childhood all the maids that came to live with us arrived with broken suitcases, expressionless faces, and gazes that brightened only when it became clear that they had found a home full of goodness. One of them was Carmencha, who hid my mother's love and her first tube of rouge in her blackened apron. The folds of that apron also hid gifts for me: fresh strawberries, sweet chocolates, and the secrets of breasts budding ineluctably in the wake of that first night of blood. This was my Carmencha.

## Afternoon Tea

Of all the rituals and food-related routines, I loved teatime when, after the sweet drowsiness and subtle fears of a siesta, we awoke to the benign aroma of coffee and milk, fresh bread from the corner store, and nana, who had left that long, dark room in order to love us. In loyal homage to the traditions brought over by English settlers, everyone in Chile—the Native Americans, the Jewish immigrants, the recent arrivals from Korea—drank sweet Ceylon tea creating a ritual pause in the day.

Tea was also for elegant ladies who, though reluctant to share a noontime meal with only their female friends, elected this ambiguous afternoon hour to do so. These get-togethers took on a rhythm of unexpected elegance, and magnificent teas were held in posh salons throughout Santiago. Opulence derived from the delicacy of each piece of cheese or cake. Once my grandmother protested out loud, declaring the food to be fit for dogs or poor Chinamen and, burdened by her prejudice, went directly home where she could take her tea as the less fortunate would have liked, with large chunks of brown sugar and fresh ham sandwiches, forgetting for a moment that she was Jewish and a well-to-do matron.

My favorite activities as a child included making up stories and shameless lies. But I also loved to listen, and to press my ear against the fragile vestibule walls. Hidden in the oldest shadows of the house, I spent hours simply listening to what the ladies said and, more importantly, did not say. The favorite topic was the servants. Many times they complained: "These damn girls, half-breeds who might as well be pure Indians, imagine, one of them, a dirty thing, asked me whether I owned a piano." They also discussed the older maids who, relegated to the backrooms, sorry and submissive, had devoted their lives to them, the ominous mistresses and their squalid children. And the ladies would comment: "She has become unbearably wrinkled and sneaky. She can barely see, and the china is stained." They said all this, and at times whispered as if revealing the deepest secret about a tiny internal illness.

I would slip away and head to my nana's room. She understood my fears, she who had the patience to braid forever, she who kissed me until I fell into mossy sleep. I sat next to her for a story about visions, the one in which mamita Susana, on a dark path, asked a squatting woman dressed in white: "Are you from the kingdom of the living or the dead?" It was really teatime when a mixture of boldo leaves and boiling water recovered the fragrance of truth.

## Women Friends / Comadres

I liked to be near them when they sat on their straw chairs, bent over the edge of time, the edge of life. They were of no particular age, of no precise time. They came from far, far away and always spoke of those distant places in the mountains, enveloped in frozen mists. I liked to shell peas and rub my hands on their stained aprons. Now I can recognize in them the smell of summer and things calmly and methodically stored away. They drank on Sundays. They bore children made by lovers curled up amid the rush. I liked that. Nothing darkened them, not sickness nor death. They always lived in the moment, their adventures uncertain. They had few belongings, usually a bent, secondhand suitcase. When the ladies who employed them turned them out, sent them to other lands, other houses on the corner, they left calmly because they had renounced permanence. They moved on in order to set their straw chairs on other sidewalks and simply talk about passing geese and the flight of birds. They moved on quietly like the very mountains that witnessed their birth.

## The Other Women

They were there, in the dark rooms, in the cracked part of the house. How to talk about them? To call them servants, small keepers of keys, enemies on the payroll, as my grandmother referred to them. But they were there, in their uniforms, in keeping with their employer's social status. The more elegant ones wore gloves purchased in provincial secondhand shops, the middle-class ones wore their hair tied back with faded kerchiefs which collected grease, dust, the odor of onions and coriander.

My mother treated them with the greatest delicacy. I don't know whether she felt that their lives resembled sad smoke and ashen lace, inhabiting other people's existence, always bent over to dust or wash, always receiving and never giving orders because they had no home. Their children were relegated to far-flung corners of the country, and bore the names of ghostly and difficult-to-pronounce bridges.

I loved them, but most of all, I delighted in observing their lives. I made notes about their movements. I spied on them through holes in the frayed walls of their rooms. I noticed that they behaved differently among themselves. They laughed out loud about insignificant things, and whispered to and touched one another in the dark. What I found most fascinating was how they prepared for an appointment with the doctor. I never saw so much joy over a medical visit, since I, of course, feared all things medical, and heard my father speak of illness as the most damned of horrors. But on the day my mother scheduled for their checkups, they groomed themselves thoroughly in the main hot-water bathroom, scrubbing their hair with lavender and camomile oil. They wore their tightest black sweaters, their most elegant clothes.

Most of the time the doctor was a friend of my father's, and at his office we were greeted with the usual courtesy, but also with astonishment at the sight of the lovely, fragrant women, all dressed up as for a party. Then the doctor spoke to them with immense tenderness, the magician, the wizard, the mediator of beloved and strange pains, of the body's omens and desires. The doctor touched them with great delicacy. He felt the tired shoulders, the hands that kneaded others' food, shucked their corn and wiped their dust from fertile and infertile ground. They did that. But now, the doctor gently tickled them. He asked them about their health, their stomachaches, and this was happiness. He came and went along their expended, tired bodies, and they smiled and were strong. They were not sick, but they needed this love, these hands lightly touching their hips and hearts.

After a stop at the pharmacy, we returned home and they resumed their chores, cleaning rooms, mislaying papers, dusting broken chairs. At night they went exhausted to their rooms in the back of the house, to their meager belongings and photographs of children conceived one bold summer night, to their radio soap operas full of characters who lived magical adventures in puffs of violet smoke, and to their lonely rest on sour sheets and borrowed time, until the next checkup when the generous doctor would gently touch their hands.

## Day Off

On Sunday afternoons, when the adults made love while pretending to take a two o'clock nap, the maids got ready to go out. "It's my day off, Magita," the lucky ones would tell me. Usually they took Sunday and every other Thursday. I liked to see them so excited, primping with passion and enthusiasm. They combed their hair, sprinkled lavender water on themselves, and in general spruced up: a touch of honey on each elbow and along each leg. I could see that they were in love with the idea of going to the plaza and buying a pair of shoes. I learned that happiness was a once-a-week stroll on the arm of a barely known acquaintance, chatting about other people's children and one's own secret passions, stored in dreams for this and every Sunday.

## Claudina

The staff got dressed up after making the beds and washing the mounds of coffee-stained cups, after cleaning the sheets on which the ladies of the house had practiced the ritual of butchers, defying time in the wake of nights full of anger.

There they were. I watched them out of the corner of my eye and I liked to see them dab a few drops of perfume in the secret roundness of their thighs.

It was Sunday, but not every Sunday, because the less privileged maids only got one a month, while the more senior servants took them all. I knew where they went and what they did because, often, as they twisted and curled the thick length of their dark, nighttime hair, they told me. Some traversed the city in order to take a bus, and then another bus, or perhaps a train that would take them to see their children who were being cared for by a good woman or a god-mother.

But their children were never with them. These children were relegated to other histories, not unlike the children my grandmother spoke about, those that had remained behind, hidden in a convent or the countryside in Europe. Like Jews forced from cities, these il-legitimate children were often turned away, thrown out onto the streets, made to disappear. Perhaps they were a darker version of my own family. My mother, my grandmother told me this. Claudina did, too, sighing as she pricked the skin near her heart with a lizard-shaped pin that writhed across her firm, exquisite breasts awakened to love.

Claudina sometimes confessed to me that she was going to see Lucho, that they met in a plaza at dusk and ate chestnuts, and Lucho tickled her palate and her ear. Flushed with happiness, Claudina told me that. Sometimes, if they went far away, they stayed in a hotel in a dizzy neighborhood and dreamed of love, spoke of love, said words of love to one another. In the distance people came and went in the streets, and they perceived the sighs of others, those less fortunate who made love in the shadows, those presages of darkness, like the insane on their day off.

Claudina told me all this, and also said that sometimes she dreamed about a small brass bed and a ceiling covered with butter-flies. I watched her, in the background the battery-powered radio sang Mexican *rancheras* or narrated a soap opera about little Esmeralda, who loved to sit by the river and had green eyes like the girls from wealthy families. I imagined Claudina and Lucho kissing one another, dreaming of love, speaking and behaving like lovers.

## A Corsage of Happiness

Claudina arrived at our house in Nuñoa at cherry blossom time, when the ground was covered with pinks and greens. She was gentle and as she walked, she pulled herself along in silence. Claudina came from the north, where the relentless sun and wind etch the inhabitants' leathery faces. Claudina's face was that of a princess accustomed to fire and to long journeys. Her bare feet recognized the eternal language of yellow dust.

Claudina liked to walk among cacti and speak with dry graves. She grew up near the only cemetery on the pampa, outside María Helena, where the dead dwell. At night, when the star-filled sky spread out like a canopy in bloom, she drew close in order to hear the dead, to feel them return home in search of the garments they wore when engaged to be married, their party clothes.

We were told all this by her beautiful, perfidious voice. She also told us how, in her small desert town, the girls had to wear carnation corsages the night of their graduation from high school. After that, they could take off for the city, as Claudina had done, to begin the arduous life of a maidservant. Claudina had been very poor, too poor to buy red carnations for the obligatory corsage. Then Claudina remembered the well-kept gravesite of a Jew who was buried in a cemetery for non-Catholics. Every afternoon someone placed two red carnations there, which quickly wilted in the intense sun and under the weight of the fogs that shaped the angry, thirsty desert.

And so Claudina decided to ask the dead man to lend her some flowers for her corsage. It took her several days to muster the courage, but finally she did it. She went to the grave and took two half-dead carnations. Then she ran to her house for a needle and thread with which to make a happiness corsage. Proud Claudina attended the graduation party, and looked radiant. Her lips were as red as love. Her gaze was like the moon, and she danced all evening with the dead man's carnations.

## Delfina

Awake very early, I felt her muffled footsteps in the kitchen. Her gait was like the beating of bird's wings, slow and simple. She was like the mist and the frost that enveloped her at the break of dawn each day. She seemed to be made of fresh, secret loam amid her clay pots. I kept a close eye on her, and that woman hugged me during nights of golden fever, helped me scare away the ghosts in which she believed. She had a face like a sacred valley, and her words, in the language of the river, were spoken only in the solitude of the kitchen.

She also saw me slip by and smell the bread she had bought the night before, the loaf wrapped in an embroidered bag. In peaceful ecstasy, I smelled it because it also had the aroma of her skin and the lost dominions of her lands. She called me "My little precious girl" and wrapped me in her shawl of frost. That's how I began each morning, in the arms of that servant who had come to my grandmother's house and later my mother's, who was and was not a present-day slave, who had a small room almost outside the house because she belonged to neither the city nor the country.

## Souls

I was never afraid of her even when her tongue became tangled and she moaned. I never thought she was strange as she bent over the earth and kissed it time and again at the beginning of every season, because she looked like ocher, reddish purple. I liked to see her slip over things, outside the whole notion of ownership and the kingdom of men. She dusted the furniture reciting lines of poetry to the divine, to dead children, grumbling, and she always preferred to be in the kitchen near the fragrance of the woodstove because there she took refuge in faith, chasms, and abysses. In that room I learned to speak of faith and the blue ghosts. My illiterate Delfina taught me the weight of each syllable and the vigor and dignity of words. She told me that everything one said was always true.

At night, Delfina was serene and very quiet. Together we would gaze out the window and watch the Southern Cross in a firmament whose stars bore the names of saints: the Ursulines, the three Marys. I was stilled and surprised by my own silence and listened not to the noises but rather the unspoken gestures of the night. Then she would say to me, "They are the souls, dear. They are the souls."

Her statement never produced wonder or amazement in me. I simply knew that Delfina spoke with the dead, and that she liked to tell them riddles and sing them secret songs. She liked the wind and its velvet sounds. At those moments she fine-tuned her voice in order to listen, and the air lifted her voice, petal of a rose from her first love.

Delfina was a sweet seer, woman, wizard, and beater of trees. I was raised near her lap and learned to smell the seasons of things, the omens of happiness. All that I am and will not be I owe to her. When I conjure her name at times I feel a nearby crackling of leaves or firewood or the water's song. I know that she is the sun who, flying high above, gives a little wink and says, "It's me, my child, it's me."

## Sacred Song

At times when the morning blended into night and my passion for life settled in beyond the hills, I would hear Delfina's footsteps and her thin voice like the empty, windy sound of a silently bleeding heart. She sang about things without words. It was the sound of ancient memories in which words blend with rivers, and rivers blend into the sky, a canvas of fish and stars. I heard her lilting, distant music, and she repeated a protective song for me. She repeated the names of the unfamiliar lands she had known as a child, places touched by her gaze, her feet. She deflected the rays of the sun as she knelt to wake us, kissing our foreheads as she used to kiss the stones in the riverbeds, with sacred fire and her people's most deeply hidden secret.

## Nape

The nape of her neck bends and unbends in a spring of lonely nights and dark rooms. I approach and cover her eyes with my hands. Delfina recognizes me because she says she bathed me and taught me the secrets of my body, from the earliest age of faint memory. I like to see her erect head, slightly tilted over the bowl of vegetables. I recognize the hands that blend with the boldo, the corn husks, the food that she chops and slices as if each piece were the secret calix of the earth's inner ear. I love her dark skin that weaves in and out of mine. That's how we begin to shell peas.

We remove them from their green cases. They are like small music boxes in the warmth of our hands. It is summer and I return to my country whose name is cloak, whose name is ashes, but there she is, bent over the straw baskets with her birdlike movements of light and sun.

I bend over her and shell peas. She says they contain the sacred stories of the lives of the dead. I like to sit beside her. Kneeling, I repeat her sacred words. Only now do I realize that she is an Indian woman. In the past she had kept her lineage like the dark, warm secret of these peas. Now we recognize one another. I am a Jewish girl, a stranger to every hour and table. She is an Indian nana, alone, occupying dark rooms in the dark space of prejudice. Her hand is warmed by mine. She says to me, "Niña, let's take advantage of this sun of love to continue shelling peas."

## Nana

I recognize her, with her braided gait, as if dragging herself along the paths of the earth to recover the broken age of her lineage. Over time her complexion has darkened. She has the gaze of deep rivers. Her face has been scarred by the sadness of loneliness carried like a fan that never stops blinking. "It is her," she says to me, and hugs me all over with those hands that, neither expectant nor wanting, make the most noble gesture of gratitude.

She washed my hair time and again. She told me stories of sleeping Araucan princesses inebriated by the clear light of the moon. As always, she promised me love. She kissed my eyelids. Time and again she returned to the plains of my ears, singing in the language of her ancestors, of fire and ashes. I cannot, nor do I wish to, explain my love for her. It was like treading the earth with bare feet, my lips sunk into the coolness of stone. That was my country: Delfina, her hands of sulphur and maize, her face next to mine, old woman and young woman braiding one another's hair.

## Wisdom

I don't know how long she has lived, how many seasons of copious rain have passed through her body. I examine her wide arms with which she washed and kissed my body, and they give no indication of their age, either, there are no tattoos of defeat on their skin. She seems spry, robust. She is wide and small like a clay jug. She was born in an out-of-the-way place, at the end of a dimly lit mountain path unknown to bad men, where days are measured by their return and the setting of the sun. She came to the city in bare feet and a woolen poncho, her eyes like windows through which she viewed the city and appreciated its transparency. She has never left those backrooms, and she has washed the bodies of little girls who never were and never will be her daughters. This is my nana. I call Delfina Mama. My son calls her Mama Ina because she also took care of him, and her arms knew that bittersweet drowsiness of his caress, that unsettled caress enveloped in mist.

My grandmother, with whom she lives, continues to tell her, "Listen, if you fix yourself up you will look less Indian." I say, "Grandmother, no matter how much you fix yourself up you will still look Jewish." The two of them have lived together, celebrated births, shut the eyes of the deceased, and yet they eat in separate rooms and use separate bathrooms. At night, the old Indian woman covers the old Jewish woman and kisses her, closes her eyelids and sings or hums. My grandmother does not understand these small gestures of gratitude. She insults her because that has been her job and her passion, insulting Indians, those who are other. Because she is white, my grandmother has never recognized her own otherness, that of a Jewish woman who crossed the mountain range to this land of the lost, full of unsettled souls submerged in solitude. Even though they come together from time to time and against all odds, an Indian woman and an elderly Jewess, each of them lives steeped in her own sense of widowhood, in her own orphaned state.

They stay together like the breath of stones, beyond time and the speed of hands. And the Jewish grandmother checks in on her, too, during afternoon naps when the old Indian dreams about the children she never had.

They both wait for me. I have returned to the house of memory, my childhood, where nothing stands still and it all comes back. I see myself as a small child, talking to myself, pretending to be in other cities, imagining adventures in ancient labyrinths. Each of them speaks to me about the other, but their gossip is not offensive. They love one another with the passion of landscapes, the eternity of rocks, and the wisdom of ambiguous friendship. My grandmother is growing ever more grateful for her loss of hearing. Her memories parade before all the absences. There is the worn red sofa, cursing time, and the old television pleasantly murmuring its own old voices. My grandmother smiles and suddenly recalls a Viennese waltz. Her memory is like that, sporadic, mischievous like a line of poetry or verse form. On the other hand, Mama Ina sits in her room and remembers the movements of the wind, the hills, and the virtues of prudence. She prays, murmurs, curses, because her mouth emits and retrieves the melodies of birds who sing sad songs. She tells me about her possessions, two or three cows and a small, sacred pasture.

They greet me, kiss me, and wrap me in the wild, mute solitude of old age, time, and silent death. But Mama Ina recognizes my body and reaches out with her hands to kiss it. My grandmother takes my hand and I see her faded beauty, the discolored strands of her blond hair. Mama Ina cries because all her borrowed children have grown, and she has been left with none. She is surrounded by photographs of her borrowed children, and my mother, the lovely proprietress who hangs at the head of the bed. I have never seen my mother so serene, and perhaps so arrogant, playing at empire in a sepia-colored photograph, a photo from a clouded time.

The two of them have remained, or perhaps more accurately, have been left behind. The poor old Jewish woman and the poor Indian woman. There is no one to save them from atavistic misery, and then I know that the only family I have in this land called Chile is perhaps that childhood that once was mine. My family is Mama Ina, a childless hollow trunk, a small, robust Indian who bathed me and taught me to taste the wind. My family is my Jewish grandmother who survived the horror and lives with little or no memory.

## Mamá Delfina

You arrive at my side this spring, twisted and lightly colored, and I look for you. I see your face, ever more set by the years. My nana, full of absence, woman asleep in the dreams of a little girl who, now grown up, searches desperately for that tenderness you promised. I look for you because no one can brush my hair like you, or sing to me in the Mapuche language sprinkled with words of Old Spanish. At your throat you wear the silver jewelry of the ancient Arauco, and you exude the smell of the rebelliousness of your land. Only occasionally did you whisper tales of the Spanish invader in my ear, lamenting the fertile land you lost. More often you prayed for me because I was growing, and you could see my bare legs predicting the threat of desire. I sheathed myself in your face, your shawl, your odor, my nana.

Today is Mother's Day and I think of you, my nana, the most mothering, yet childless, guardian of the memories of others, collector of First Communions, of lives other than your own. Today I invoke you so that your memory might join that of the dispossessed, so that the Araucan land will not be a fragmented sentence. I want to tell about your saints, intercessors between life and death, and how you crafted vestments for angels and offered me herbal tea, how your hands resembled the braided wood of your forests.

Fear vanishes when I invoke your name. You are always there, and when I call you, nothing is impossible, there is no more anger. I sit beside you and your voice, not innocent but serious, cries out for your land and what no longer is, because you, Delfina, get up every morning, kneel on your timeworn shawl, and give thanks for the earth and the storm. You call on all your transparent ancestors, before tides and rains, and there you are, lady of the hills, lady of my memory, my nana, mother of mothers, yet always my nana, rider of rivers.

### Carmen Carrasco

Carmen Carrasco smelled like smoke and cilantro. Her entire being was the color of evening ocher. She was about beginnings and the preamble to nighttime magic. Every afternoon at five, the appointed hour of nostalgia, she began to hum certain songs from the southernmost regions of the world, songs that smelled like birds and clouds. Carmen Carrasco was like the south of Chile, powerful and remote, always distant. She liked to sit on curbs worn away by the history of lost times. She liked to listen to the silent footsteps as the city too took on the color of smoke puffs, and time became as gray as the cloaks of lovers passing by undetected in the mist. Then Carmen Carrasco turned her attention to gossiping with friends. After spending the entire day in the interior patios, the neighbors came out, and like Carmen, sat down. When the evening fell it was time to go outside, to gather at the corner, to laugh and to prolong the early autumn or the thickly fragrant spring on the curb.

Suddenly, on one such smoky afternoon, the earth opened. Terrified, Carmen Carrasco told us that the dead were hungry and needed to be fed. My frightened sister and I ran for her lap, feeling the tremor deep inside her. Her legs, wrapped in thick, ocher-colored hose, suddenly became thinner as we rushed in her direction. This was the 1968 earthquake, and the first time we heard the neighbors desperately scream the word "God" instead of "Christ." I saw Carmen Carrasco make the sign of the cross and pray silently. A few times I heard her scream the exquisite word "Mercy."

The earth opened up, and for seconds that seemed like centuries, we dangled over the abyss. The cemeteries boldly decided to make a fresh attempt at life, and frantic gravestones danced an insane dance. At that moment I was afraid and felt my mortality. I couldn't find my mother, who by chance had gone to visit the dead. I was eleven years old when I found out that we are fragile, vulnerable, mortal beings. Carmen Carrasco hugged us and prayed, and I secretly pronounced the invisible name of God.

## Baptisms

Carmen Carrasco was afraid because we had not been baptized. One Sunday she took us to the church on the corner where we were known to all as the neighborhood Jewish girls. This long-ago label no longer strikes me as odd, nor provokes my anger, because it carries with it neither malice nor hatred. They simply called us that because we were those strange children who never had any new toys to show off on December 25th.

Carmencita took us to the church, and we raised our foreheads for the very sweet, foreign-born priest, who softly murmured over our moist heads something like a hymn of love and a request for God's peace. From then on, like the real little girls in the neighborhood, I too loved churches, poetry and incense, blue and reddish capes, the world of the host, and the softness and violence of the divine cross. Truly, the synagogues were opaque, full of too many shawled men wailing and bowing, beating their breasts. I wondered whether their chests might crack open from so many hurtful blows.

Following our baptism we learned the Our Father and Hail Mary. We memorized the saints' birthdays and celebrated each special eve with beautiful abandon. My mother never judged our comings and goings along the merciful roads of Catholicism because she, too, secretly loved the amber of the golden churches.

## The Burning of Judas

Carmencita, arched like the inhospitable roundness of the wind, said: "Come, girls, unfasten your hearts," and off we would go, dizzy with sleeplessness, crazed by sudden happiness. At night the streets of our familiar neighborhood seemed inhabited by the face of strangeness. There they were, the maids' children, burning Judas figures, and saying, "This was done by Jewish traitors, Jews as big as bonfires." We were afraid and the hunting night, in love and out of its mind, fell on our lips. My sister and I did not identify with those enormous Judases, but we suffered on account of that tiny star that came loose and left us reeling with the same sense of shame we felt whenever we saw the dead body of Christ tied to a wooden cross.

## The Little Souls

They were there, at the edge of the most sinuous roads, like small boats of feathers and wood. They looked like little houses with diminutive cupolas and candles lit in gratitude and surrender. These were the little souls, small sanctuaries, reminders of those who had died in a violent or unexpected way. A little house at the edge of the road was made for them, recalling the spot on which they ceased to blink, to wonder at the world.

As a child I liked to stop at these chapels. Sometimes, without knowing who the deceased was, I offered weeds, fresh herbs, and shoots for good luck because my nana Carmencha assured me that someone should always take care of the dead, speak silently to them, and not leave them submerged in the sloth of oblivion.

I always kept the custom of sprinkling other people's graves with water and visiting cemeteries, for it is there that true stories are found, in the funeral rites of a people. In order to preserve these customs and traditions, I was told countless stories, like that of the orphan bride who, dressed in white on the day of her wedding, went to the cemetery at midnight to chat with her dead mother.

Sometimes I think that the whole country of Chile is a great forest of little souls, a cemetery sliding into forgetfulness. And the little souls cry at midnight, or at the break of dawn, when no one visits them. And the little souls get angry, their gentle light shines on an ever diminishing number of vigil keepers. They know that the whole country is one large cemetery for the living as well as the dead, a few slippery tombs in the cracks of oblivion.

## A Cat and a Chicken

Of all the gifts I received as a child, I remember the dead animals poisoned by sinister, demented acts of cruelty. My first gift was a beautiful, small chick named Pepo from the south of Chile. Carmen Carrasco brought it to me from her beloved province of Chillán, where she traveled the hills with a cart full of flowers. It was a wild chick, uncared for, and shared the fate of those born under the star of dispossession. So Carmen Carrasco packed it when she returned to the capital. In her bag she carried every southern smell, a multitude of herbs to cure stomachaches and lovesickness, ward off the evil eye, improve one's breath, and understand the nighttime constellations. Amid the boldo and cilantro was the chick, a nauseated sleepwalker upon arrival in Santiago, yet a member of our household for a year. It grew, and at times pretended to be a grown-up bird, flapping its wings on my shoulder.

The first day of school I was served a lavish lunch. Hours later I realized I had eaten my chicken. The knowledge that I had consumed its flesh meant that I had blanketed myself with death. I had betrayed that which I loved. I feared for my lips, my mouth, and took pity on all the animals devoured without compassion. From then on I learned how to part with things, to know that time makes eternal, skeletal moves, and little by little I realized that nothing is really ours. Carmen Carrasco confessed to killing the chicken because she claimed that such were the rituals of life. That which brings happiness also brings cupboards replete with languid pain.

My other lost animal was my cat, Pimpín, a gift from my friend Noemi Rothfeld. That blue and white cat regularly urinated on the roses cultivated by our grouchy neighbor, a lover of quarrels large and small. One day he decided to put poison under his loveliest bush, Pimpín's favorite. When my father came to see us at the beach, he brought the news of my beloved cat, poisoned. That night I dressed in black and cried for him. During nights of insomnia, when I try to draw near to what has been lost, to recover memory, I always dream about my cat and my chicken, the most valued animals of my childhood in Chile.

## Protection

I longed only to hear her, to sense the sound of her footsteps in the deep night, made darker by the secrets she deposited behind pieces of wooden furniture, behind the shadows frightened by her presence. I could tell she was coming by her fragrance of moss and lavender, by the shawl tucked across her ample, white-flowered bosom. Then, before nightmares or migraines swept me across the savage, solitary night, pulsing with celebrations of nearby death, she would return, and pray over me as if kissing my forehead, and her breath mingled with mine. She smelled of meat and the threadbare kitchen. I was her little girl, she called me her "niña" and she smelled of certain rivers, pillows, and silk pajamas. I loved her in order to hide amid the beating of her wide, always blooming heart, and even in her dark room lined by dust and rain. Seated at my feet, she prayed for me, for my sister, for my parents. She said, "My God, how unlucky that this child should be Jewish, may our Lord protect her." And I also loved that lord evoked by Carmen Carrasco during nights of celebration and insomnia.

She told me to call my angels by their names: Estefanía, Eduviges, María de las Mercedes. I followed her advice because through her I discovered the goodness of simple women who watch from the sidelines, women in chairs along the sidewalk, those who dream of a roast chicken or roast pig as a special treat on their saint's day. Sweet Carmen with a voice full of dragonflies and steel, who handled a thimble as if it were a dream, who knew how to protect me from terror, from my own secrets, who saw me naked, and with a smile let me go outside to taste the rain.

Now I want to hear her. Now I want to return to the kitchen. I want her to let me wrap myself in her apron of cilantro and cherries, and to hear her tell me a story of the prince who was really a frog or girls with hair as blond as mine, because without my nana I become confused, my childhood melts away amid these fast-moving days, during this time when the air can only be felt with fingertips. If she would only say to me, "My child, it is good to live without haste, it is good to spray river water on your skirt and to think about love." She is not here during the day, although I must confess that at night I hear her firm steps approach, copper leaves in her hair, her apron as blue as the sky. She sits at my side, kisses my eyelids, and says here I am, niña, you can go to sleep now. And my hands are small lights that illuminate the sailing of my restless body.

## Bread

Suddenly the bread appeared on the lush table. It was the bread fetched at dawn, the illuminated routine of every dawn, the bread made by Juan who had to get out of bed even before Nana in order to make it. Every night, as I yearned for bread, and grew sleepy in your boldo scent, you asked me how I would like my loaf: in the shape of a heart or bird or yuyita flower to gladden my palate? My entire childhood I thought about two things: generous morning bread, adorning the meals of the wealthy and the poor alike, insinuating the fragrance of a well-stocked house, and the poetry of Gabriela Mistral. Now, in this northern land, so far from the things I love, there is no fresh bread, no boldo. There are no dreams of dawns lightly sprinkled with flour, now but a memory, and your face amid the shadows, dear Nana, but the pain of absence, forever gone.

## With the Nanas

The night became a dark, insinuating painting, and doors closed. It was the season of mint, so the dead took seats to wait in the shadows amid the coals and tea leaves. Carmencita Carrasco arrived at the room of dreams, where she, too, seemed to lose her way among the old but always diaphanous photographs. She slid along, heels clicking, her feet used to foreign lands, earthquakes, and hurricanes. She arrived wearing a blue shawl, potato plasters, and a cigarette tucked behind her ear. Seated on the edge of our bed, she began the ritual that shaped all our nights until we came to North America, where there was no one to keep us company as we entered the realm of misty dreams.

Then Carmencha kissed us and smoothed our tangled, mischievous hair. To us her hands were not those of a servant, they were hands that protected the health of all the sick people they cured. Carmen Carrasco began her usual litany: advice about love and death, the perversity of hatred. Most of all she told us to be kind to strangers and to act charitably toward the poor, because one of them could be an angel. We read many stories on Carmen's face which reflected all the tremors she had survived, each fissure and crack she had seen in the surface of the earth. Whenever it opened, the earth bore her name. Carmen sang with a voice as tenuous as a flame, a stream flowing day and night. In her shawl she carried a drawing of the stars and imaginary animals.

When she left Santiago, heading south with her cart and two burros, her sewing machine and transistor radio, I did not cry for her. Instead I cried because I knew that no one would watch over my dreams, no one would sing to me like a stream. I was alone without my Carmencha and her golden thimbles, my Carmencha who believed in angels, and whose mouth produced words like beautiful pieces of fruit, like moist, wise clay. Each night her shawl protected me from fears both great and small.

Whenever the night is a perverse desert, I call out to my

Carmencita and ask her to assure me that among strangers I will find my guardian angel.

## The Backrooms

I liked going to the backrooms. I wanted to loose myself amid those shadows that separated my house from hers, the house of the rich from the dark little rooms of the poor. Hers had the sort of light that comes from deep within, and there were candles, crucifixes, love herbs, and Virgins in golden shawls. She also had a painting at the head of her bead: the portrait of a child as an angel, with violet-colored paper and a papier-mâché golden crown. One day somebody told me, in anger, that the boy in the picture, her son, was illegitimate, but I didn't care. I wasn't interested in the dead boy in angel's garb, nor in the torn photographs misplaced in dark albums stored in a worn drawer of a blue straw dresser.

I liked her, her smell, her patience. She played with me when everyone else was in a hurry, too busy to pretend. But she was there, profound and happy, slicing beans. In a small opening blessed by light, she had planted boldo and mint in a tin can. She gave me herb infusions and hot water when my stomach felt rushed and overwhelmed.

That's how I spent my childhood, in the backroom, beside her photos that didn't portray her life but mine, the lives of children she had never raised. The cherub presided over this party of strangers' portraits, because she, too, was a stranger whose first language, not Castillian, had been ripped from her tongue. They made her feel ashamed of it. Sometimes I heard her whisper in my ear a few words in her own language. She wanted me to store them in my memory, and from those words I fashioned my hymns.

For many years I loved her more than life itself because she conquered danger and was a source of peace and faith in my almost empty house. Now she has become even more enigmatic. She shuns noise and ostentatious questions, yet my own children go to those backrooms where nothing has been moved, where only our images have grown high along the shadowed walls. She plays with my children, shows them how to plant, and tells them that by merely closing their eyes they can sink into the love of the earth. My children love her as much as I. They yearn to be at her side early in the morning, and at night when the wind and countless dead relations teem between the mirrors and the shadows of what once was.

She is made of wool and stone. She is infinite, impervious to her own pain. She is like the earth, never closing the door on us. She tells us that when she slept beside the river as a child, she knew secret words.

Part 2

# Journey to the Other America

# Chapter Five

# Time of Ire

## Autumn and Lovers

Autumn burst onto the avenues with its foggy rings. The leaves were a long, flooding river. The leaves were like long stories, still unwritten, walking drunk. We would go outdoors in autumn as if in search of an orange celebration. Unexpectedly, the warm afternoon would surprise us with its ochers and happy sounds like splashes of holy water.

My sister and I would go to the stand where chestnuts were sold. In our hands they became as fresh as spring water, as happiness. Suddenly we caught sight of the lovers in the park. They were leaves, cascades of leaves. There they were, motionless, turning their hands into rings like rivers, like leaves. We saw them kiss as well, and their breath seemed like clusters of mist.

My sister and I dreamed that one day we, too, would be like the lovers in the park, lost in the contemplation of a painful, agile kiss; that we would fall in love in a park near our house, where drunks and lovers played. But the fierce war years arrived, and we left our homeland, and we didn't experience love, not in Spanish and not in the park.

## Israel

The fragrance recalled things and times of war. Gardens and debris, a time of ashes and voicelessness. In the distance, the blind man hung his head, worn out beyond the billows of smoke. But I loved that land. To my grandfather, my nana Carmencita, and the corner butcher, Israel Hazbun, it was the Holy Land. It belonged to all and to no one.

I arrived in Israel in 1973, ten days after the outbreak of the Yom Kippur War. As they saw me off, my parents trembled for fear that my young life, as uncertain as the spoils of the war itself, would be cut short. Nevertheless, passion and longing convinced them, and me as well. I survived every trial, and at all costs.

It was my second trip to Israel. The first had been to stay on a kibbutz in the peaceful hills of Galilee. This time I arrived alone at the airport, now devoid of larks and electric lights. Taxis were scarce, until I met a Hasidic family from New York. The women's heads were covered with translucent scarves and the men's beards seemed tangled in nighttime and stars. The children were like miniature adults. Distant and lost, we set out for Jerusalem.

Unexpectedly, one of the family's suitcases opened in midtrip, and spewed its contents onto the highway. No one became upset, and we continued our journey in silent composure. When we caught our first glimpse of the hills of Judea, they cried with me. I cried not because I was approaching the golden walls of Jerusalem, not because of my solitude, like that of the wounded, but because there was no rest to be found in this landscape. The earth opened up to drink in sadness.

Suddenly, beyond the hills, plumes of smoke belonging to all my ancestors reached toward the sky. I had arrived in the Holy Land. Birds covered the firmament and words were draped in absence. Someone said, "Peace be with you," and in those words I heard the voices of the rabbi of Santiago, the village pastor, and the beggar in every plaza. "And with you, too," I replied, and I knew I had found my second home.

## Jerusalem 1973

During those months of war I forgot language and signs. The alphabet balanced on my timid tongue. War made us forget the faces of our childhood and our parents. At night I uselessly drew paths to all the possible houses and I banged up against beheaded objects along the red roads. During the days of war I forgot my own garments and my mother's party dresses. During the days of war, everything was like a fog waiting to ambush us, and there was a tumult of voices that spoke, and at times there were no voices at all in this holy city.

## Moshe

My skin and hands were warm. I liked to rest my hands in his rough ones, and at times I kissed them so that he would let me hike through the hills, rivers, and meadows in the heart of summer. I rested my head on his knees. Between his tired legs he kept a rifle. He was my first love, a soldier with hazelnut skin. His name was Moshe, and he whispered words of love as well as words of war. For many months I dreamed about him. Then I would awake, and travel for hours to lay beside him. I was only sixteen.

He visited and revisited my body, with its girlish imperfections. His mouth rested on my waist and his hands, held by God, were a melody. I loved his intermittent silences, his sudden starts in the brief night.

He covered my body with poppy petals and, in the language of my childhood, traced words of love and desperation on my skin. Every wartime night I covered him as he lay beside me. During long nights I called his name among secret stones and in the very secret held within my body, like the thirst of an opaque and clear sea. I expected nothing more than his warm body next to mine, and his table full of wheat and philosopher's stones.

Suddenly, as I returned along the indomitable paths of Jerusalem, assaulted by the surrounding season, he was stretched across the bed near Death, to whom he had returned. His feet were increasingly dark and his fingers became tired swarms of blood. He searched for my face and in his I glimpsed the passage of agile death, the one sought by young men at war. We kissed for the privilege of life. The kiss belonged to a time that was so ours, so ephemeral, beyond naked bodies.

His hands grew thin within my hands. I delighted in drawing the sound of larks, balconies tied to the sky, and seagulls. I was only sixteen when I met him. I had moved to North America where I felt no one loved me or my accented speech, nor my lost memories. But I spoke to him in Hebrew, the language of deserts, war zones, love, and in my own life, Chile. I loved him. Paused between his parted lips I said his name time and again under the Jerusalem sky. He was my first love, and I still remember the warmth of his legs like a path, kneeling beside mine. When I kissed him, the birds of death were afraid, and fled his sad mouth. "It's you," I told him. "You have returned from the Golan." And in my drunken happiness of all things related to love, he recognized my face and my hair. My hands restored a fragile semblance of his life.

## God's Place

And if God was everywhere, I saw him in misty places, beyond language and spells. Sometimes I felt his breath behind the bewitched cast of my glance. I liked his passions as manifested in this true Paradise, Earth, and not in the darkened crucifixes on the bedroom walls of lonely women.

Neither haughty nor arrogant, this God allowed lust and excess. He let children eat chicken breasts, not just worthless wings. Perhaps my God suffered less than the one on the cross, ripped open, blood on his temples, his torso painfully curved. My mother said there was a god, but for me he had no name, no borders. The God I imagined was like an island, solitary and set apart.

## The Balcony

Suddenly, from the Hotel O'Higgins, just outside my grandmother's balcony, we saw the U.S. Marines, the Chilean Marines, and we heard the words: "Stay in your homes. This is a state of siege." My grandmother said that they had killed poor Salvador Allende, who had been her boyfriend in grade school. He used to say in his magnificent voice: "History makes a people." Those were his last words. I leaned over to hear him more clearly. Someone said that his palace was in flames, and that no one could be happy ever again. Now I remember that moment, on this afternoon of fire and ash.

Salvador Allende was a doctor and my father's friend. When he died, we left. No one threw us out. No one blindfolded us. But we knew that a life of gags and fear was pointless. That's why we left, to no longer be from a place of gendarmes and repugnant dictators. Suddenly night fell and, tired, we learned the names of other cities and other lands.

## White

The day the soldiers arrived to fill every space, I dressed in white and went outside. My eyes were the white of peace. I did not want more war on the sidewalks. I did not want cities to become impenetrable cells. Dressed in white, I offered each faceless pedestrian a white handkerchief, a square of love bathed in light. My hands were like the white gauze of dreams fulfilled.

## Curfew

Beyond the darkness lie all the forbidden zones. The fog knelt among the avenues, the concealing fog. Slowly, with a perturbing stillness, the streets emptied. Desperate, I saw the figures, opaque muzzlers, mobilize in silence. No one remained in the city of the living dead. No one remained in the parks or on the wide boulevards. Suddenly the angels of death appeared, draped in enormous capes of black steel, their pupils askance, their nostrils flaring like those of apocalyptic animals seeking the perverse heart of the wicked night.

That was the hour of curfew, when nothing and no one remained, and the sea folded back into its own lap of dead snails.

## Dark Silence

We gradually sank into the darkest silence. Gone were the light and our composure. Fear gripped us like an insinuating fog, like an implacable fire. Fear approached, then stood at the foot of our beds and asked us to account for our lives. At that time we were too young, amazed, and deluded by our own splendid and defiant youth. We lost our ability to speak, because speech was forbidden. Our souls and our hearts left clandestine tracks. We lived in secret in order to touch with our hands, to feel. Far outside ourselves, cities were ransacked, children and old people were arrested. Slow women and those who moved quickly, desperate women and those who were mad, eagerly searched for the truth. They searched for their children and forgotten old people. Night became long, like a rip in cold silk.

We lived a story that was not our own. They made us disappear against our will. The dungeon occupied every space, every dimension of fright. In that way we became weak, small, solitary. We didn't see, look, or help. Our hearts broke, and the truth fell into a dark well, a rhymeless dungeon from which there was no escape.

## The Texture of Fear

History has the texture of fear, of moans in the vague night, slammed doors at dawn and barefoot men tied up, leaving their homes with frozen feet and blindfolded eyes. This story unfolds in certain neighborhoods of the city where not everyone sees the sinister darkness. Sudden knocking on the door, the mother shivers with fright. She asks them to leave her house, says that her son, daughter, nephew, granddaughter, dog will be back soon. The mother awaits the homecoming with the hopefulness of those who return, and no one comes back to the country, and the streets fill with what is forgotten and memory is like a secret noise or the murmur of kisses prior to flight.

## Disappeared

They called to me before the hour of silence, on the edge of time, before darkness covered the room with pain beyond what is tangi-

*My great-grandmothers, Helena Broder Halpern (left) and
Sonia Drullinsky. Helena was born in Poland and moved to
Vienna at an early age. In 1938 she left for Chile to join her
son, Joseph Halpern, in Valparaíso. Sonia was born in Odessa
and arrived in Chile in the early 1900s. They were good
friends, speaking with each other in Yiddish. My daughter,
Sonia Helena, is named for both of them.*

*My nanny, Delfina
Nahuenhal, and I
on the seashore on
Isla Negra in the
late 1970s.
Delfina, who raised
me since I was
seven, still lives in
Viña del Mar with
my grandmother
Josephine Halpern.*

*My sister, Cynthia, and I with Marcelo and Saul Stein, celebrating my fifth birthday in the garden of our home in Santiago.*

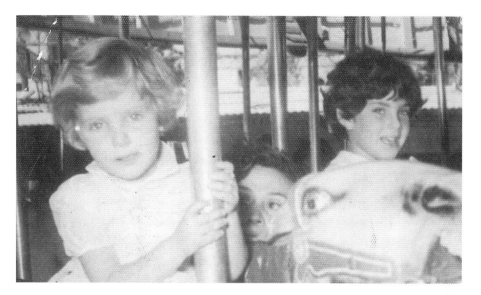

*Cynthia and I on a merry-go-round in downtown Santiago, 1961. In the middle is our nanny Maria.*

*At our summer home in Quisco. Cynthia is nine; I am about seven.*

*Picture taken about 1972. I am hugging my beloved history teacher, Marta Alvarado, at the Hebrew Institute in Santiago. She died in 1991 in a nursing home in Santiago.*

*I am a fourth grader at the Hebrew Institute in Santiago.*

*My son, Joseph, during a visit with me to the home of Pablo
Neruda on Isla Negra, looking out on the sea as Neruda did every
morning. My son, Joseph Daniel Wiggins, was named after my
grandfather Joseph Halpern.*

*With my children, Joseph and Sonia, and my husband, John Wiggins, summer 1998, at Chataqua Institute where I taught poetry.*

My maternal grandparents, Josephine and Joseph Halpern, at my parents' wedding, June 19, 1948, at the Hotel Carrera in Santiago. Josephine was born in Buenos Aires and Joseph in Poland.

Here I am in 1988 in Bahia, Brazil, with my younger brother, Mario Agosín, and his Brazilian wife, Teresa Ferras.

*Fiftieth wedding anniversary celebration of my paternal grandparents, Raquel and Abraham Agosín, in Viña del Mar. My grandmother was from Odessa and my grandfather from Sebastopol. Almost the entire family is gathered here; I am on my grandfather's lap.*

ble. It was like breathing very deeply, knowing that later there would be nothing but absence.

They arrived in my dreams and called to me. They had my grandmothers' names, or perhaps my own, but they asked me to find them, to submerge myself in those disappeared women of Latin America who also inhabited my dreams. They approached my covers, and like faithful companions in death, they slept with me.

The years I spent in North America coincided with ferocious political transformations in Chile, Argentina, and Uruguay. At the time I was only fourteen, but at home it was whispered that people were crossing the Andes disguised as nuns. Others fled to the Caribbean where they invented new names, new pasts. I was safe in a house made of wood surrounded by enormous pine trees.

Yet my destiny joined theirs. Perhaps I had also disappeared. No one could pronounce my last name without breaking into laughter, no one knew who I was. I myself unable to feel at home in that lost territory where I had been set ashore and abandoned.

The nightmares of disappeared women coincided with my personal terror. I knew that I would never go home. I would forever be lost in every city. The keys to my hotel rooms would not work, and no one would let me in. From windows I would be spat upon.

## The House

At night, when the warmth of bodies becomes diffused with the darkness, when dreams entwine with the sound of nearby breathing, I thought about the locks in my house. The memory came slowly but was clear and translucent. I felt as if my body were levitating, rising from the surface of the bed with agility and returning to the doors that seemed to have lived an entire lifetime in devoted consecration of the memory of those rooms.

And then Carmencita Carrasco was there with her ash-stained shawl. All the grandmothers were there, like fairies seated at a roundtable that called out to souls. There were those lovely women I never met, yet I knew that their heads had been shaven and that they had filed nude through the tunnels of death.

Everyone is at home. Those who saw me asleep and tucked in my dreams, and those who I never saw sleep but nevertheless inhabit my dreams. Beyond the locks are the interior terraces, because every-thing that happened in that house was like love, turned inward and secret, visible only to those who knew how to see, those with sor-ceress eyes. My room faced an enormous red-tiled terrace, the color of the earth, ocher colored. In the mornings the southern hemi-sphere sun came in strong, generously, and threw silhouettes across the glazed surface as I pressed my cheeks against the warm bricks.

The garden beyond the terrace, with its medlar trees, lemon trees, and damson plums lying on the ground. Once in a while the ducks and chicks strolled by, the animals that I cared for and also ate as a child. There they were as if life and time were but a reconstruction of a real past, and only in that garden, veiled in dreams, was I able to recover an image of myself: a happy child, surrendered to the rhythm of her body, the fragrance of wood, the aromas of poverty and abundance.

I found out that if they blindfolded me forever and filled my soul with dust, with pain, I would still find the sublime road home, where pleasure and folly and the hazard of devils were the times of ire and happiness in a chiaroscuro world.

Upon returning to the time of vigil, I left my house, its locks, morning noises, sidewalks and rose water mirrors, the knife-grinder who had lost a leg and the night watchman who returns to his beloved darkness. All that and I know that I can remember the names of the stars. For each name lost, I recover a star.

## The Wind

At times the wind travels across my dreams, my face. I sense the fra-grances imbued there, and the stars travel random paths of chance. Memory disobeys as it seeks to penetrate more deeply into the soul. On those nights of fleeting time I return to the house where, in my father's lap, I learned to read. I recognize the room where my brother slept as a newborn, a gift to us all in my parents' maturity. Sometimes I wander down the long hallway where the smiling clock keeps track of false seasons, flights and returns, lost souls. Everyone in that house moves, sighs, and I recognize Delfina's soundless winged footsteps, heartrending, the footsteps of poor women, those who clean up after others, bring order to others' lives. I stand there alone, in awe of life's pulse, its very essence.

Then the wind seeks me out in that place where I no longer belong, my house. A faithful traveler, I am passing through. My lips leave tracks as I move on to the red brick terrace always warmed by a generous sun. I see the hands of Julio, the gardener, "el maestro" as we called him, bending toward the earth. Passionate Julio teaches me the happiness of cherry trees, wakes me with a bouquet of daisies. My house smells like a village, and I love everyone who ever lived there. On those nights of imaginary frontiers my heart seems to bleed as I struggle to find open doors. A rude person has changed the locks. Clothing floats, elongated like skeletons in the tenuous dark of night. Homeless, I long to move back into the house where we were happy, where we smelled of hyacinths and stories. Memory unbuttons dreams about what I was, what I could have been in that house, if only the soldiers had not come with hands like claws and faces of death.

Where is my home and my city, my street and my friends, that little girl who was not permitted to grow up on her patio?

# Chapter Six

# *Pilgrimages*

## The Gringos

"The gringos are here," said my grandmother whenever the rains threatened to flood Santiago, and blond, robust men who looked alike distributed blankets, cups of coffee, and bottles of ketchup, laughing like John Wayne in the movies. They were the gringos, men with insipid faces but nonetheless good people. That is what my grandmother said, constantly amazed by the American propensity to wear strange-colored hats.

But the Americans came to Chile not only in response to natural disasters. They also showed up when they did not like a certain president, or industry could exploit barefoot populations even further, or doctors needed to test disturbing drugs. The blood of poor Latin Americans, especially women, seemed convenient. These were the same Americans who distributed blankets, played at Peace Corps volunteer by day, and at night trained the torturers.

These are the Americans. They are no longer governments without soldiers, but men, people like us who clandestinely torture and incite dictators to silence us forever. My grandmother feared them because she understood that those hats were stinking war helmets, and there was no charity in those insipid eyes. With their doctrine of national security and their hope for democracy, they brought only misery, a hunger for power, the exploitation of the weak, of bare-foot, pregnant women.

## Exile Begins

The night we fled was quick. The Andes mountains, like a giant mother, released us. The stars seemed to touch the very soles of our feet and caress our shoes, the shoes we had worn during games of heaven and hell.

We boarded the Lan Chile plane in a hurry. Out the small windows we could see all our loves: my history teacher, Martita Alvarado, in her worn, garnet-colored coat, my classmates holding the flags of Chile and Israel, my green-eyed grandmother, and my nana Delfina, whose eyes were like hazelnuts. There they were, and here we were, creating boundaries that have never been dissolved, creating that inevitable separation between those who stay and those who must flee.

The sky and the sea made unexpected noises. We were nowhere, we were from nowhere. Our journey had begun. My mother thanked her dead grandmother for life, and asked for her blessing.

## To Set Foot in America

As if quizzing a tourist, they asked me what it was like the first time I stood on American soil. I paused, allowing my memory to pick up speed, or better said, to appear barefoot in my own language. It was 1974, in Savannah, Georgia, after a long journey in which exile invented a path to other cities, became accustomed to the strangeness of things. We traveled from Santiago to Buenos Aires, then to Mexico. From there we went to Atlanta and then to Savannah, where we were met by a kind man, a friend of my father's. He was a foreigner as well, born in Greece, an immigrant to the United States.

The descent into the American landscape was for me a mixture of wonder and enchantment. There were trees and benches to sit on at the airport and people with unfamiliar faces who greeted us. The enormous trees surprised me, their silver beards swinging from remote crowns. I was startled by an unlikely amiability, hardly consistent with the image projected by television shows.

Our arrival was marked by the throb of all immigrants. We felt we were passing through. Rather than living life at that moment, or configuring the meaning of becoming a citizen, I was seasick between shame and love. I could see only the faces of my friends, of beggars, of the man who sharpened our knives, the maids in our neighborhood, their enormous bags of freshly baked, aromatic wheat bread. I felt as if my body had split in two and my dreams had been divided. It was in Santiago—not Savannah—that I awoke each morning into chilly air, flung open my windows, and greeted the Andes mountains.

My arrival in America was wrapped in an enormous blanket of cold, a veiled uncertainty. My English was hopeless. The few words I had learned in school, where language instruction had been a mere diversion, fueled my confusion. Coming to America meant it was impossible to feel attached to things I loved, and little by little to begin to love what was strange, those trees with dangerous beards, for example. I felt cut off from nature. I had to reinvent myself and explain over and over who I was. I was obliged to tell my story and to say: "They did not throw us out of Chile, but we had no choice if we did not want to live under a dictator."

Gradually the story became tired. The inhabitants of Savannah, and later Athens, Georgia, became used to the sight of us. We posed no threat, had good manners, and were very white, almost Nordic in appearance.

But increasingly we felt alone, shaped by a peculiar unease. We lacked a community of beloved people and things. We had no history, continuously starting over beyond memory. We did not leave, however, and over time got used to being foreigners, the dimensions of benches and the sizes of clothing. We learned to master this foreign tongue that would never be ours and that grew increasingly heavy and uncomfortable. Our words took on unfamiliar rhythms when they wanted to sing and scream in Spanish.

Whenever we returned to Chile, our friends there would smile and say, "Here come the gringos. You must be having a wonderful time abroad." For me, exile was like a piece of cloth that never took shape. It could not be embroidered over and over again because it faded, fell apart, lost its color and texture. Exile was a well of perverse and enchanted memories, yet I never said so to my relatives in Chile. I kept quiet, just as I did in Savannah and then Athens. I knew I was a foreigner, a stranger, a tourist by vocation. At times I did not even know where I dreamed or made love. I did not understand the meaning of provisional time. Above all I learned that for us there was no way back.

## A Foreigner's Nights

At night there was no fragrance of moist grass or jasmines. At night there was no one in the streets. Where were they? Why didn't they come out to converse with the freshening eve? Where were the grandmothers like Carmencita who convened curbside, unevenlegged chair in hand, greeting both friends and enemies with great gestures of reverence? Where were they? In front of the turned-on television, solitary and sickly. And the empty night, sad and sublime, its aroma of jasmines, the dancing skirts of the night, existed only in the songs of my pain.

## The First Months

Our first months in America were hardly memorable, wrapped in ominous silence as they were. We had left behind more than our language, food, familiar flowers and herbs whose names I knew. We felt the anguish of an assassinated president and a palace, a country in flames. Later I understood that those who disappeared from the face of the earth were my age or a bit older. While my generation disappeared, we exiles disappeared as a family. In those initial months after we left, we ate in fastidious silence. Any gesture or word irritated my parents, who desperately tried to consolidate a new life at almost forty years of age.

The new food tasted sad and we lost our appetite. We missed strong coffee and the special taste of Chilean milk, bread, and butter. To lose flavors is to lose one's soul, because the flavors of food are like the flavors of memory. My mother got used to murmuring, to sighing as if the weight of her words was painful. News from Chile was bone chilling, prisoners, missing people, three classmates disappeared, one shot to death. The Jews who supported Allende left for Israel. We withdrew into a corner, into the mouth of an abyss.

For several years I did not understand the ethical and social reverberations of the disappearance campaign. Beyond the mounds of youthful corpses was the impulse to eradicate ideas, flowers, promises. My entire childhood I had woken up in the middle of the night to images of trains and men whose flesh had been cut. Now I awoke feeling like a woman gagged.

We lived in what was supposed to be one of the planet's truest democracies. Yet talking was dangerous. I was a foreigner, hardly anyone was familiar with our story, and no one associated Allende's fate with the CIA or US intervention. To people in the north, Allende was a communist. I constantly had to explain about my country, how our civilization was much older than that of the United States, how we loved one another and were legalistic yet realistic about our laws. I wanted to say that we were a heroic and good country. I spent years trying to explain to my classmates who we were and why my family was here and not there. I have finally understood that despite my years of effort, they have never been able to understand me.

## The Flying Squirrel

At night, in the stone house in Georgia, sadness parched my throat and fear overwhelmed me. Where was I from? Where was my uniform, my little sack of protector stones? How had my life vanished from the pink patios of my house? I shut myself in a small wardrobe with a flying squirrel, indomitable and distant like my sadness. To what extent I heard my mother desperately calling my name, searching everywhere for me, racing frantically to the garden as if summoned to things that are dead.

Much time has transpired since those years in Georgia where they made fun of my height, my accent, and my Latino and Jewish background. Almost twenty years have gone by, and only now, gazing sleepily, do I write about that time. Here I am in the final days of the short, narrow month of February, a benevolent month in this winter of good omens. I have traveled far. I left the narrowness of Georgia and its banal prejudices. I arrived by chance at Wellesley College, home to steep and noble buildings and women with rebellious hair. I came here because a Spanish woman loved my poems and the shrouds of my sadness. I walk through a forest of fleeting leaves. It seems as if spring was in a hurry to make its triumphant entrance. I have learned the names of the trees and the stars of the northern hemisphere. I have improved my accent and I no longer hide in wardrobes.

## Berkeley

The first place we had come to in America was Berkeley, California. It was 1960. The myth and legendary stories of California gold became real. Every inch of the sidewalks did indeed shine, but as I stooped for gold, I retrieved only small chunks of pavement. Little by little I understood the old saying "Not all that shines is gold," and America stopped shining. Life was rather tedious and premeditated, regimented. We who loved noise had to be quiet after ten o'clock at night, when the people in the apartment below turned off their lights to watch television, or tortured us by thumping the ceiling with a broomstick.

Not all that shines is gold, said my grandmother. "Golden America" gradually changed color. It became darker, more ocher, and we decided to return to Chile to avoid persecution of folks with foreign names, folks who smell bad, or who are fat. We returned to the south where there were no sparkling streets, but many shining rivers, flowers, and conversations with strangers who, astonished by our blond hair, said all that shines is indeed gold.

## Memories

The nights grew long with the insensitivity of insomnia and at times my mother devoted herself to contemplating the faces of our dead relatives, the photographs. She would name them amid the vast silence. Nothing belonged to us, not even the few pieces of furniture, on loan from bad neighbors who went through the motions of seeming generous. True generosity was too dangerous. We weren't in a poor neighborhood or a ghetto, but because we belonged to that restless group, immigrant Jews, we knew what it meant to be from such places. We were from South America, and we loved the Spanish language with a passion. In North America we learned to moderate our passionate, spontaneous expressions of love. We learned to be other than ourselves, and I, at fifteen, attended Clark Central High School where they mocked me. Every day I came home to console my mother, weeping over the piles of letters she had thrown on the floor. The kitchen pots were always empty. There were no fragrant rubber plants, no kites, and my father became ever more fragile and quiet. That is how I spent my days, years that blended into immense nights in Athens, Georgia, a southern town where all who are different are mocked.

## Clark Central High

My first days at school in Georgia come to me in a fog. As a shy girl from South America, I did not speak. I could not understand how they did math, took strange measurements, subtracted, understood time. Protectively, I wrapped myself in an immense green coat and yearned for the three o'clock bell when I could finally go home and caress my mother's torn face while I taught her Shakespeare's sonnets.

## Mr. Watson

His name was Mr. Watson, and his face was that of a greedy man of limited intelligence. He liked to talk about immigrants, dates, and the relative merits of various skin colors. He assured us that the Germans were spiritually superior because of their blond manes and their excessively blue eyes. Then came the Italians, the Irish, and the dirty Latinos. Intrigued, he looked at me as if nature had made a mistake, as if my nearly white hair and my accent should have been Germanic and not Hispanic. That was the real Mr. Watson, soccer coach, friend of Georgian ancestors who whipped blacks or donned hoods to burn their homes. He was my first history teacher in Athens, Georgia. He terrified me, and I missed my history teacher in Chile, tiny Marta Alvarado, who told me that real history is made by the people.

## At First

At first they invited me to the movies, to munch popcorn. I seemed odd to them, but perhaps exotic as well, and a halo of privilege descended on those who spoke to the girl from South America, the girl who was not from a slum and was white. My accent made them laugh out loud, and besides, I was blonder than they were.

So I tried to imitate them. I chewed gum quickly, sighed as loudly as a locomotive, but I was not myself. Like a bad dream, I confused languages, and switched alphabets as if changing the rhythm of my skin. I was never invited a second or third time, and decided to befriend other foreigners, the third-class immigrants, as Mr. Watson, the Georgia high school teacher, called them. Nevertheless, I was happy among the outcasts. We told one another the names of our cities, and exchanged our grandmothers' recipes. In the strangeness of southern Georgia, where the nighttime streets seemed strangely empty of people, we felt like a family of crazies, speaking various languages and naming the trees of our respective countries.

## Halloween

I wanted to belong, to feel that some of the girls loved me, but they only said: "In America we don't drop by people's houses without calling ahead." Distressed, I looked at them intently, but could not understand the rituals or codes, and had no place to hide. Suddenly, on Halloween night, someone invited me to trick-or-treat in the neighborhood. I remembered the Day of the Dead, when each home, including the Jewish ones, contained an altar of dreams, an offering of peaceful doves. Here they asked me to dress like a witch, and go out into the Georgia night, which was like a balm made of strange oils. The night was heavy and dark like a fermented fan.

I put on a witch costume. I had small pumpkins spilling from my pockets. I was happy because someone in America wanted my company. Suddenly it began to rain. The black netting of my costume stuck closer and closer to my body. One look and people closed their doors on me. They did not love me because, in truth, my face, cracked and split, had shut down. I had become an intense and painful black presence. On that first Halloween night, when fairies and witches ventured forth, I was as strange as they were.

## The Amusement Park

One day my mother decided to take us to an amusement park so that we could finally have some fun. Yet we did not feel that the park belonged to us. It was full of enormous people, whose excess weight knew no mercy, dark figures thrilled by the wheel of fortune that would be theirs for only a brief instant. That amusement park seemed like a horror show to me: semidrugged men and women coming and going as if their only possible obligation was consumption. That afternoon, outside Coniers, Georgia, I knew for sure that my happiness lay in sitting with my nanas in light, floating straw chairs, watching the street, the world, the characters pass by in shabby old cars, loudly hawking bottles of colored glass. The true wheel of fortune was to be found in the contemplation of things because life was in the streets, in people greeting one another, in winks of the eye, good evenings, and the hum of ferocious crickets.

That night we went home wrapped in silence. No one was waiting for us. The plastic chairs echoed in the distance and the only memory was my hand marking the entrance to that amusement park with gloomy blue numbers, like those I had seen in the hands of my Omama Helena when she placed her white gloves on the warm table in Vienna.

## The Immigrant Girls

We got together after school each day. Our expressions were those of bewildered larks. Something united us, perhaps our clothing, always a bit too long and awkward, never eccentric or colorful enough. Or perhaps our eyes, fixed beyond the horizon, those dark gazes tinged with stony wind and ashen moss. What were we back then? How did the students at Clark Central High School in Athens, Georgia, see us? I only know that as we passed them in the hallways they threw spitballs at us. I only know that they told one another, "Don't talk to her, she's Latina and a Jew." I also heard them say, "Don't talk to those other two, either. One's a stinking Pollack, the other a starving Irish girl covered with rotten freckles."

That was us, the immigrant girls, girls with accents who wore their hair pulled back like sprays of stars, and yet there we were, together at dismissal time, standing in the most painful, shadowy corners. We had formed our own clique, the Immigrants' Club. We swapped recipes, survival advice, and of course, we somehow got through it. Today we are all part of the great luminous, rotten American Dream. But at what price? What price must an immigrant pay in order to triumph? Only now the survivor has neither questions nor answers. I survived, determined to find a new life in a foreign land, that nighttime ocher that will always belong to others. Suddenly the immigrant sees an unfamiliar face pass by in the middle of the night or on a sunny beach. She sees herself, and in that victorious moment of recognition, she finds herself, and her new country is the old one where everyone says hello and the wise earth awaits her.

## Neighbors and Friends

They called themselves my friends. Of course, one must keep in mind that they were not the friends of childhood. I knew neither them nor their parents or siblings. They were part of this transitory society in which people move very often to a different house, city, or job. Permanence was unheard of, and staying in one place was viewed unfavorably. I longed for the time when things were settled, when venturing onto neighborhood streets meant recognizing the trees I had been viewing with passion since childhood.

I wanted to make friends. I opened my house to them and offered them the disinterested face of love. Sly neighbors, at first they offered me the intimacy of affection, and I considered them genuine. But friendship became an exchange of favors, and often an abuse of my good will. I watched their children, made their lives easier, entertained them with my stories of apparitions. The neighbors thought I was their servant. After all, we were foreigners. They always said, "You are so lucky to be in this country," while I thought how unlucky I had been having to leave behind my light, my street corners, the care of my nanas, my friends' riddles.

Then they would move to a new neighborhood, emigrating to other houses far away, and I would no longer see them. I stopped hearing from them and lived cut off, wondering why they had left my life as quickly as they had come into it. But they said that's how life is in this North America, so fast and daring, changeable and unfamiliar. I was left more and more alone in my house of stone, and I took refuge in the palace of my shadows. This is how I lived, distant, longing for those durable things that were mine, that had the texture of permanence and that lay buried in the time of lost spaces.

## Of Parties and Other Audacities

American parties never cease to amaze me. First of all, it is very difficult to have them, because people take out their enormous planners in which they record dates and times, each second of the day, the moment at which the fall leaves change, or appointments for making love, the days on which they ought to pray and eat a bit of butter, and wink at Mr. Cholesterol. As a result, only among the cracks in busy days are parties allowed. In general, nobody has them for any particular reason because having fun in America is so complicated. There are certain procedures and structures. In New England it can even be considered bad taste to laugh out loud. Laughter should be decorous, under penalty of death. One must uphold a certain level of elegance, and one's laughter should sound neither like a waterfall nor like a flute.

Parties are held two or three times a year, and there are all sorts of them: parties to sell plastic containers known as Tupperware, to sell gift wrap, for fat or thin people watching their weight. Parties are always held for a specific reason, and one invites people instrumental to that purpose. In short, a marketing principal operates between the person giving the party and those who come or don't. For example, the plastic container parties are attended by housewives; Garden Club parties are for the town's aristocracy. At these parties people stand, holding tiny glasses of white California wine, and small plastic-looking chunks that are in reality pieces of cheese. They greet one another with restraint, talk about the best rug shampoos, and their lack of time to make love, although the latter activity is said to be good for the circulation and one's complexion! They say goodbye, promise to call, then never see one another until the following year when they repeat the same conversations about yet a different rug shampoo and even less sex, and some even more efficient way of imagining life has been invented.

Parties in my homeland are held on a daily basis. Laughter is free as sunlight and people gossip and are happy. They laugh out loud and from the pit of their stomachs. Nothing is too cautious, nor structured, and happiness is something like breathing: constant, fragile, hurried, slow, but never methodical. There are no luxurious displays of ostentation. Many times I have seen knives used to make music, and people dance in a state of drunkness, because words have not yet lost their souls.

## Borrowed Furniture

Mute, sliding through the empty house, around furniture loaned to us for a week at a time, we looked at each other like lost people at a crossroads. We thought about leaving, but the idea of flight came after dark when the noise of imagined trains could be heard in the distance, and everything we loved seemed to have gone the way of that sound, trains moving through ghostly towns.

Dawns were painful. We could not find the words for water, love, grass. Our foreignness was a barbed-wire fence running through us. Then my mother decided to go to the temple, not to pray nor to become wiser, since she believed God was in one's conscience and in the memory of the just. Rather she thought that we might join the temple in order to become part of the community. My father, distrustful of organized religion, resisted. Nevertheless, we women of the house disobeyed him.

One Friday in autumn we headed for the Jewish Center of Athens, Georgia. The brevity of the service surprised us, yet the social life was pleasant, made colorful by little cakes and juice served in plastic cups. Little by little people spoke to us, and confidently assumed that we Jews from Latin America came to the United States in search of better refrigerators and home appliances. We were not asked about our rituals, our songs. Conversation dropped off as we drank from those detestable plastic cups. And that was how we discovered that the Jewish community was not very interested in us because, from their point of view, we were third-class Jews. We were neither from Europe nor from Russia, we were not in fashion. We were poor Latinos who only by a twist of fate happened to be Jews.

No one loved us at those latitudes, neither the neighbors nor the schoolteachers nor the Jews. This was the America, at once marvelous and sinister, that gave us the opportunity to remake our lives and kill our souls.

## The Piano

We knew it, but my careful, sweet mother never told us that there was not enough money to buy furniture for all the rooms. So there the piano stood, in the most immense solitude, drowning in pain and slow music that seemed like gusts of wind tied to the mouths of the dead. My mother told us that nothing would be put in the playrooms, where we had only to close our eyes to see the things we loved. I imagined my hair being braided by nana Carmencita's fragrant hands, rubbed in jasmine, and I imagined songs in Spanish as I looked for my school shoes, the ones I had worn crossing lawns and stones. I yearned for my uniform, my bag, and I knew that my dresser full of memories was empty, that our solitude was overwhelming, and that in the room of discoveries we were alone, my mother on her knees watching the sky which was not ours either, and the wind howling across the faces of the exiled.

## The Georgia House

I looked out on the perverse darkness of woods that were not ours. We missed the immense Andes mountain range, the canopy of the southern skies, familiar to our skin and predicting rain. We went out infrequently during those months in Georgia, only in search of used furniture for the empty livingroom devoid of friends, the immense grand piano assuring my father's marvelous eccentricity, intact despite arduous journeys.

One day a group of faculty wives, the spouses of my father's colleagues, invited us to lunch. They were all named Mrs. John Smith, Mrs. Maurice Sullivan. I thought it strange that they had male names, and shortly thereafter I found out that when a woman marries, she not only loses her last name, she also officially acquires her husband's first name. The women at that luncheon were neither elegant nor genteel. They lead rushed lives, anxious to recite the infinite number of chores that validated the futility of their exaggerated suburban existence. Suddenly one of them, referring to my mother, said, "They had to leave, they were thrown out." My mother lifted her darkened head and said, "No one threw us out, we decided to come to this country. My life changed significantly, my standard of living dropped, as did my moments of happiness and leisure, but no one threw us out." Then, slowly and with the dignity of the just, we said goodbye, returning to our house of stone, our empty livingroom.

That afternoon we cried as we held one another. My mother told us that she missed daily words of love, her neighbor, the man who sharpened our knives, the woman who sold bread, and her recipes for happiness. From that moment on I knew that this country, the shape of its trees and the way its citizens behaved, would never be ours, but that Chile would not be mine either because memory became tangled, and was sometimes as cloudy as the autumn sky. I got used to not having a country, to my own linguistic confusion, and to lighting my grandmother Helena's candelabras in the dark. She brought them from Vienna to Chile and now they were in the Georgia house. The light of those candles marked all possible home-comings and the silence of prayer revealed the city of memory, wrinkled in the breath that does not yearn.

## Fissures

In Georgia, at night, I examine the cracks in the walls of this old house. I am not sure where I am, or whether I am dreaming. Sleep slips away into dark spaces. Someone covers my eyes, prays over me, or blesses me. Then the other woman who lives in this house arrives, and on my forehead she traces the sign of the cross. That's what my nights were like in Santiago, but I am not there with my omama Helena and my nana Carmencha. So many blessings during that enchanted childhood, so many storybook gardens. Now in the Georgia house I hear my mother sobbing and my father, in the distance, playing the piano. In this house of stone our only callers are the mailman or a neighbor who comes to complain or tell us that he fed our dog poison.

The fissures in the walls of this house surprise me. They have no particular shape, they don't resemble anyone's face. They aren't of a particular time. Suddenly I look at the foot of my bed and I see my shoes, and next to them thousands of misplaced shoes, dying shoes, shoes filled with the presence of lost things. I can't take my eyes off the pile of my dead aunt's shoes. Then the walls take on the fissures of smoke, and the room fills with hair and fingernails. I don't know where I am. They have come for me. I, too, sob, echoing the sobs of my mother. No one reaches out to me, no one offers me a shawl. I am here, on the other side of love, alone with dead people's shoes, with the cracks in a house that has no name.

## Gardens

My mother loved her garden. At times it was a murmur of lilies, at others a windy caress in her gaze. My mother arranged flowers according to their names which she repeated: poppies, anemones, gladiolias. She never allowed a single flower to die in her hands.

When we left Chile, the garden was left spinning in dry disarray. It lost its voice, like a country bleeding in the dark. We left on a trip, but our destination was uncertain and distant. My mother filled a tiny bag with fresh earth. She said it was to ward off fear and to deceive sadness.

In America we did not have a garden. The flowers had different names. Our names changed, too, little by little. People recognized us by our accent, and in dark and hostile tones, asked us time and again where we were from. Far away, I said, very far away, where flowers and fairies have similar names. In America, at the age of fourteen, I discovered that I was not white, but rather a woman of color. It had nothing to do with the shade of my skin, but rather with my voice, the obstacle to being like them, dressing like them. "Woman of color" was the tattoo born by every foreign girl, unchanged, alone on the walk home from school, a stranger to all, the target of spitballs at recess. Woman of color, they called me years later at the university, despite my golden hair. My husband was told, "Don't get mixed up with her, with that Latina." They still did not know I was also Jewish.

Woman of color. I repeated that phrase and it became encrusted in me like a song, a ceremony, a talisman of silences and rarities. But when they spoke of color, I thought of my mother's hands, praying like two islands, distributing and working the earth in her garden, arranging flowers like poems, by name, allowing colors to create their own ceremonies, to strike their own wild balance.

For many years, when I was lonely because no one wanted to play with me, because no one invited me to their home, I thought about my mother's garden, and how her feet blended with the poppies, how the golden pollen threaded my hair with the fragrance of the countryside and peace.

I couldn't understand America and America couldn't understand me, but she left me alone. I was generous, tolerant, and she, malevolent; I was hospitable and she closed her borders so many times, yet I stayed here because perhaps I knew that the true garden is in the secret palms of beloved hands, because the garden is in the kiss of peace, in the language that calls flowers anemones, violets, and lilies.

## Magnolias

In the afternoons, when the stupor of rain became increasingly thick and humid, Mom and I would venture out of our stone house, our house of memory, to hear the wild crickets in their monotonous and defiant songs. Above all else we loved to stroll through the park carpeted with magnolias that emitted clearest fragrance into the thick air of the summer night. Outside of the house, we inhabited unfamiliar territory and asked ourselves again and again where we were, to what strange place had my father taken us. Suddenly we noticed the magnolias resting on our skin, warm with a nameless texture, and my mother said, "This is your Georgia, a park, a mother and a daughter in search of distant and transparent voices." And the splendid magnolias were our guardians, our great companions during aimless, insomnolent walks. We had finally understood that when they said come see us again in that sweet southern accent, it really was not true, and when I appeared unannounced at the neighbor's door, no one came to greet me, no one wanted to play. Head hung and shoulders slumped, I would retreat. But I could always dream in the afternoon, and dressed all in white, I would find my little piece of Georgia, my magnolias that would forgive my foreign ways, and that would always happily inscribe my skin with the fragrance of love.

## Letters to Be Answered

Silence is all around us. Things exist in silence and there is no one to question about memory. All silence is opaque. It hangs its head, like jewelry plundered in a war. My mother dreams of her garden and its flowering peach trees. She dreams of the yellow and purplish aromas of her country.

Our lives are governed by letters. My mother devotes exclusive time to them in the late afternoon. She enters a stony space of silence in order to write letters. She inhabits the letters she receives, and kisses them, but she always writes more than she gets. Suddenly I see her fragile body bent over the cloth. I see where she keeps the letters written to her. I see her writing that solitude and silence are necessary for nostalgic thoughts. At times, when she looks around for her jasmine-scented tea, I try to read what she has written, but there are no details. She relates our daily routine. She speaks of the garden and the constant death of her yellow roses, so different from the ones that grew around our home in the south.

My mother writes about us and says that we are strange in our new language, our gestures tedious, trapped in a coil of foreign words we cannot pronounce. At times she yells at us, then puts her arms around us, gently asking forgiveness.

Every day there are letters: some arrive, others go out. They all demand answers.

## America and My Mother

My mother was in her early forties when she came to America. She had a very thin voice and laughed like a firefly. Most of all, her words seemed absent and yet, when she spoke in Spanish, she seemed to sing. Once in a while I would see her lying down on her hands like flowing rivers. She stroked my hair as if she had returned to the wild and good time of childhood. Sometimes her gaze sunk into empty space. Then she took out the old, wrinkled and worn photographs, and brushed her fluid hands against them. My Magita, she would say, this is your great-grandmother Helena, and this is your aunt Leonora, lost in an Austrian forest, and here I am, wearing my string of pearls on my first trip to Buenos Aires. These photographs were sheer happiness on those lonely afternoons. Somehow they belonged to us because we had already lost our past. I saw my mother become thinner as she gazed at the photographs, and I pinched her arms. We did not know where we were or what year it was, and a strange fog entered the room, a heavy breath like sadness, distant and re-mote. Then I kissed my mother, spoke to her of the sea, and rested in her eyes, the ports of each of our happy journeys home.

## Wanderings

My mother no longer frequented dreams nor did she laugh ecstat-ically after a glass of red wine. The displacement had wrapped her in silence. She wore unusual expressions, and in the placid strangeness of her face I understood that her eyes, violet ports, had become opaque, like pedestrians traversing foreign and frightening cities at night. When I asked her about Chile she folded her face like a moist canvas. She remembered the rubber tree near the middle of the garden, and the flowering plum. That was the past that had remained suspended, awaiting a possible return, someone to tell its story. But what sustained the past? The past was a forest buried in the shadows, amid faded debris. Our past was like an uncertain pendulum. Everything has been readied for our return, but we never went back. We took up residence on the borders.

## Georgian Soil

The earth extended itself like a plateau of red textures. One had only to touch it, to rub a generously extended cheek or hand over its surface to know that it was a creator of food. This was the reddish earth of the South at the other end of the world. And the men peered outside to delight in the setting sun, which wearied of shining all afternoon on a people who only a hundred years before had been picking cotton in bare feet, their backs still bearing the tattoos of all their ancestors. They had come to America as chattel, purchased with a few gold coins of avarice.

In Georgia I approached the rhythm of the English alphabet with the singsong accent of a river, like the speech of everyday folk, and in this landscape brimming with tranquil beauty, they told me that I was a Latina and a Jew.

My body was a burning flame. There was no possible refuge since my country was a barbed-wire fence. To whom could I talk when I saw my mother imploring an unfamiliar, ever more absent God to take pity on her alien condition. Suddenly I remembered the red earth of Scarlet O'Hara, who always said "Tomorrow is another day," and I went to the nearest field to coat my hands and my cheeks, my entire face, with Georgian soil. In that way I felt less like a fugitive because perhaps the breath, the eternity, the incantations of life were there, in the earth of Georgia, like a pencil plowing my future.

## Country

My country is the rain, a time of defeated branches, a sound of ghosts
and bones walking amid the shadows and memories. Always my
country: a strip of land, moist like my mother's lips when she was a
little girl in the south of Chile and hid to watch the other girls splash-
ing each other barefoot in the transparent downpour. From a distance she watched others make little rivers with their feet and dead
leaves. But she, my mother, loved the rain as she dreamed within
her wooden house in a town of strange friends.

In New England now, I love the rain like someone loves a scar,
and I dream about it. I imagine what my country once was—a sealed
labyrinth among the araucanas, a wounded, moist tree trunk.

Not to have a country, a bit of land, was like a delicate fear, at
times furious, crawling along my skin. The fear meant living in imaginary landscapes that had probably never been seen: late afternoon
in the fields beyond the drizzle. At times I closed my eyes to feel my
skin. I imagined that all the dead were with me. I named my great-
grandparents, my aunts kidnapped by the delirium of blue gas, and
only then did I sense that my country was that which I had loved. To
forget was impossible. Oblivion added humiliation to the torment
that had been war. For Jews, oblivion is high treason.

Little by little I became accustomed to not having a country. As
time passed I dreamed less about it, but I did dream about my own
naked body lying on the grass, and then I dreamed I was in a garden where my hands gathered tender flowering roots. Then I knew
that I had come home to the garden, to the merciful earth, keeper
of bones and memories. I discovered that my country was an orchard, a lemon tree, the dahlias in my hands.

## The Exile

The exile does not begin to write about her new city. She doesn't
read poems in foreign languages. The exile seems obsessed with returning to her old city, where she can once again imagine and invent
it, traverse its broken sidewalks, profoundly wash its earth, trees,
rivers. Perhaps leaving the place you call your country is like being

a single tributary of a confused and turbulent river. The exile does not cling to her new country, she concentrates on remembering the old one. That's what we all did when we reached this America, at once so beautiful and sinister. I was only fifteen, could not speak English, and did not understand why we had left our house, our patio, the butchershop on the corner. Nevertheless, there we were, behind closed doors, not knowing whether we should learn to move to the accelerated and incongruous rhythm of our new country. So we lived as if trapped, inventing other rhythms, inhabiting a universe of postcards bearing names of other cities that perhaps we had known. We made them ours by leaving that broken world behind. And yet that old world peered into our lives like an obsession, a constant presence in a new world that did not belong to us either. Nothing was ours any longer.

## Wellesley College

And I came here, to these towers, to this lawn beautifully tended by the generous hands of ladies devoted to the art of gardening. I came to Wellesley College because they had told me that they liked women who were eccentric, solitary, angular like lost angels from Paradise on Earth.

Back then, the vertiginous disorder of words delighted me, and though I did not wear a black cape like poets of previous times, nor recited nighttime prayers throughout the city, I was a poet. A poet who was neither thin nor eccentric nor rational, yet I already bore the title that allowed me to enter this university of brave women, beautiful women, triumphant in their good work.

I sent a small envelope by mail to a Spanish lady, Elena Gascón-Vera, who, without knowing me, decided I should teach here where Jorge Guillén, Pedro Salinas, and Vladimir Nabokov had taught. I said yes, of course, and the names of those great men seemed to me divine. That was how I began to make my home in this paradise for women, fat and thin, sinuous and angular. I like the silent walls, at times too frozen to kiss, yet they remind me of the grottos where I place my cheek, rubbing into it the moisture of ancient vines.

What is between these walls, in this forest where women do not fear their own spirit and come together to study standing on tip-toes? Perhaps it is for reasons of love, reasons of power and knowl-edge and ambiguity, for love of the ability of language spoken by women, for love of being heard here, our voices audible, no longer an echo in the darkness.

To love is to anticipate the future with the wisdom of good bal-ance. The language spoken here is free, limber like fire. In a certain sense this is the city of the women of Christine of Pisan. This is the city of Sappho, where there is no fear of the alphabet, where we name and unname ourselves, and love one another, always.

I came to Wellesley a fearful girl. I am still a girl, but now I am brave. I have not stopped writing. I have not stopped loving. I always recognize myself in the towers, and I approach them in order to keep the memory of all the women who could not speak. That is why I am here, even though I am not from here. I am from Africa and from plundered America, I am from Harlem and from Bombay, but I live here in Wellesley where I create the signs of the stars that illuminate my lost sisters.

## Russian Lady

Her name is Matilde Salganicoff, a princess's name, a Russian lady. I saw her and wanted to know more about her large violet eyes, her hair of smoke and copper-colored mists. She was an oak from nearby and distant Argentina, a country next door, hemisphere neighbors, because one need only cross the Andes Mountains to get to her city. But Matilde is also one of those modern refugees. In-stead of a loaf of bread, she carries a diploma, yet still feels like a renter, a transient.

When I saw Matilde I thought she was an aunt of mine who had come for a visit, to keep us company, chat, laugh, and gossip. In her unbreakable Buenos Aires accent she asked me whether I, too, felt transparent. Since then Matilde and I have been friends, sisters, fugi-tives from an uncertain destiny. In her I recall any given cousin of mine, a schoolmate, those familiar voices that I had left behind.

I met Matilde not by chance, but because I was willing. She was like my Aunt Eduviges or my grandmother Sofía. I loved her because she was tall, radiant with the majestic dignity of those who have suffered and escape unharmed from battle. We recognized one another as emigrants, women without a country, without borders, emigrants from countries like an empty language. She told me that at first, newcomers are like tourists, curious and amazed, but by now she had become transparent, invisible to others and to herself.

Matilde speaks of her country, but it is neither a city nor a river. It is the forest that grows in the fissures of her heart, a paradise of wild birds. Matilde does not want to return to what came before because she is wise, accustomed to losing things, names, and borders. She knows that nothing is truly ours, and that a country is a smiling garden where women walk alone, as in books and in life. Perhaps that country is a book yet to be written, a highway of women talking to themselves each in her own language, a garden with roots coming undone, like hair, like sanity.

## *Matilde*

I

Always watching
the snow file by the woods behind my house
that perhaps is not my house.
It snows as we approach
the millennium,
this could be Prague or Berlin
or the Low Countries
because at the end of the day these are
foreign lands, Matilde.
The beautiful snow is no more than
exile for the deaf.
It snows, Matilde,
and we are not in the south
and our hearts beat, unaware of what they miss.

II

It snows, Matilde, in strange countries, and the
flakes

are beautiful in their slowness,
like the breath of God
playing with the fragrance of
transparent air.
It snows, Matilde, and the trees
seem to be marvelous animals,
suspended in whiteness.
I tell you all this, Matilde,
because this dazzling snowstorm
reminds me of perverse afternoon
lights
or the wonder of children in the presence of
their own bodies.

### III

I speak to you of the snow, Matilde,
so as not to feel so alone on this white horizon,
there are men without homes tonight, Matilde,
and women alone resting against the transitory peace of a
        window.
It is snowing in New England,
Matilde,
the fields are like
white deserts,
shadows dilute shapes
everything is so remote in these thicknesses.
Dreams, Matilde,
are not ours,
because we are from the south
and we do not believe in guile
or haste.
How distant this landscape, Matilde,
unrelated to our
lively and unwary skin.
It has nothing to do with our words
which create a necklace of happiness
each time we meet.
It snows, Matilde, in New England,

and I would like you to come
so we might walk together on this
transparent, indifferent
snow.

## *Snow*

The snow with its privileges of silence, its white austerity, the hush of horizons, is beyond time. There is nothing familiar in this immobile landscape. The light of the air is sharp, the trees are like small animals suspended in the beauty of the snow's threads. The immoderate white is so beautiful. Tonight it is snowing urgently in New England and in those cloudy mirrors, too white and brilliant, I do not recognize myself. Has this now become my landscape, or have I adjusted to it? In what lost dominion did I leave behind my shadow and the southern wind?

It is snowing in New England, all night long, and I wake up thinking about the Pacific Ocean, as beautiful as a phantom, knocking at our windows during nights of leisure, when my sister and I pretended to celebrate the rituals of the tides. I live in New England and dream about the Andes Mountains, the wild summers, the bursting fruits, the generous melons. I teach at Wellesley College, one of the most prestigious universities for women in the United States. I came here by a twist of fate, a spin of fortune's wheel. I prayed in this new land without knowing what to say. A Spanish magician loved my poetry and without ever having seen my face nor studied my family tree, she invited me to teach here. This is where Jorge Guillén, Vladimir Nabokov, Pedro Salinas, and Alice Walker taught. Were they happy in this place that preaches love and communion, yet views foreigners, people with accents, suspiciously and with subtle contempt?

Perhaps Wellesley College represents the privilege of teaching and living in America, with a stable salary, a relatively open intellectual culture, yet it is a somber place. I have been here fifteen years and I cannot say that I know my colleagues, nor have I opened my soul to them. Neighbors acknowledge one another but are afraid to shake hands. Calm and indifference are the hallmarks of proper behavior. I never laugh with them, drink until midnight, or bare my heart. I live warily, terrified to say what I feel, afraid I will always be judged. I have felt less like a stranger among the college chauffeurs and groundkeepers than with my colleagues. Though the latter wear the multicolored mask of diversity, they are enemies of those who are different. I come from a world where words are songs to be sung out loud, where the sea revives the soul, and where life is almost inexplicable, hybrid, strange.

Yet I have managed to find happiness. That is, I have had moments of happiness in teaching, in solitary walks around the unchanging, beautiful lake. I have never felt a part of the campus with its ivy-covered buildings. I have been, and always will be, "a stranger in a strange land."

## *Laura*

Laura came into view like a coastline, amid chaos and unpredictability, in the tangle of forgotten dreams. One day they told me to call a certain novelist in Maine, and I did. Her voice was measured and tormented like that which emerges from water, then becomes even more watery, mobile, a season of peace and faith.

I loved and love Laura just as I did my friends from Chile because our conversations led to the truth, to wonder regarding what goes and what can be seen beyond time and sound. With our words we fled the shadows, looked at each other's inner self, never the outward one. The river of time stood still and voice became a poem, atemporal and with its memory intact.

With Laura I found my lost country. It was in her hands like rocky cliffs, in her gaze at once near and distant. We shared my childhood and hers, our adolescence, and she spoke to me about her city so that I could enter it. I told her about the light dresses I wore as a girl, made of tulle and organdy.

With Laura I returned to usurped childhood sites, spaces covered and uncovered. In this way I did not forget happiness, and I found a friend, foreigner by vocation, whom I can tell all that I see and hear in the dark, about the tearing noises, the trains going nowhere. And there is Laura, dressed in black sea foam. She picks up the perversity of my dreams and says to me: "Linger on the horror, listen to the voice, feel the foreignness. You cannot live without looking at the depth of things."

I linger with her and she catches up to me, headed for the shore where the sand is phosphorescent and in motion, where silence is a joy and she is on the seamless horizon, powerful and sovereign.

## The Raft Girl

She had the face of an uncertain traveler, as if her gaze could only rest on what was already distant, as if her fragile body was only used for the memory of what is most fleeting. We approached each other like people who see a familiar face in the fog. I thought I had come upon the threshold of memory. When I was her age I combed my hair in a way that hid the shyness of my young face.

We said hello as if we had traveled together in another life, and she told me about her crossing from Cuba on a very fragile raft. She told me how, inebriated, they traveled aimlessly, letting go of dreams, inventing what would be a possible future in the darkness. What did you eat? I asked her. "Nothing but honey," she said. "We got to America with salty honey on our lips. But now there is no more honey here, only news of sealed doors and the predictions of foreigners." She asked me how books are made, because she wanted to create her own, about her crossing. I told her to look for green ink and to lace her story with red string, and to keep a cup of gratitude on hand. "I believe that is how books are made," I told her, sobbing.

We looked at each other and in her face I saw Havana, Sebastopol, Odessa. A refugee girl is like a child of war, pulling her hair back with ties of many colors, armed with wild lanterns so as not to get lost, not to forget the way home. Refugee girls tell the same story, undertake the same crossings, drink honey and eat bits of sugar, live in silence. Refugee girls write and, in the solitude of parties, recognize one another, sit together, their legs crossed, close their eyes, feel their way around the open houses they left behind.

## Molly McArthur

Stories of flight, of people in disguise crossing sinful rivers and borders covered by ocher-colored shadows, these were our stories. Perhaps I could only tell one story because life was like that, a single story, a necklace of words, hung on the string of destiny and happiness. The stories were always about flight. They had the rotting fragrance of cities, the taste and body of women anchored in the oddest ports. Then they told me how they crossed through the forest.

All the stories were about flight, strange birds, and desolate omens. But then you arrived, Molly McArthur, with your hair of red windowpanes like fire and ash. You, Molly, still so young and so close to your dead. Your story was also about flight. You told me things. You told me that you carried a blue notebook under your arm in which to keep the story, like a person putting away a tablecloth, collecting drops of rain and amber, or thimbles overflowing with sadness.

Your story, Molly, made me think that perhaps all stories are stories of sea voyages and returns, of flights, of time and love that never come back. Molly, you spoke to me about your great-grandmother who was known as Breeze because her hair seemed to predict the direction of the wind, the thinness of the night.

You told me that she had traveled from the coast of Italy, from Sicily to Greece, hidden in a box spring. That's how she arranged to flee the voices, the rubble, and wars. Molly, you told me that she seemed like an angel suspended in the most restless silence on high, that no one recognized her breathing, her body amid the veils and the frost, all the murmurs, all the debris of war. Your great-grandfather did not groan, he merely carried the songs in his gagged mouth, around his shackled wrists. His silence was that of those who survive and love life.

That is how your great-grandmother got to Cyprus, with her body enfolded in dreams of strangeness. As she traveled she dreamed of her children and finding a time of peace. She dreamed of the living and the dead, her gratitude in the face of the void, in the face of being born or not. All this you told me while I stroked your hair of red autumn leaves, of flames in love after the rain.

Your great-grandmother survived, she married an Englishman

from Cairo who showered her with jewels and tiaras, built her imaginary palaces and the most beautiful bed made of bronze and flowers named for all the cities of the world.

I too survived, Molly, listening to the stories of my great-grandmother Helena with baskets full of chickens and silver padlocks on the Vienna doors. I too survived thanks to the story. Then I knew, Molly, that everything has to do with seeing the flights and the irreverence of time.

## Birthday

Yesterday I turned forty-one, and I felt distant from everything around me: the house, friends, my children, the daily routine, it all made me feel impassive. I thought that if I were to cease to exist, few would remember me. I did not envision my burial, but I felt increasingly remote and worthless. Rather than approaching a future filled with uncertainties, my thoughts clung more and more to the known: the past, my grandparents, my house, the steep street, my air. I have been in America for more than twenty years and I cannot forget that I am not from here, nor can I forget the anonymity of this vast country that does not allow me the sense of truly belonging. I feel the presence of what we were, of what, as foreigners, we left behind. I feel it as if in a language of fragments and dreams.

Today I remember the room in which I lived for many years in my parents' house. From that room, facing the rear terrace, I enjoying the sun rising through the bricks. I enjoyed feeling the rain framing the night. I looked forward to my mother's birthday and Carmencita arriving at dawn with an illumined cake.

## Mama

Today I thought about you, Mama, and decided to write you. You were forty-one years old when you left your beloved house on the corner, although at times you were repulsed by the smell of Don Juan's singed meat. But this was your house, Mama, and all of ours as well. You liked to return and go in because on the outside it seemed ochre colored, invisible, devoid of light and wonder. But when you went inside, secret hallways appeared, enormous reddish terraces and the trees—orange, plum, and lemon—that you planted when I was born. I am now the same age as you were then, Mama, forty-one, the age when you left the house, handed over the keys just as Omama Helena probably did in Vienna, and you left. You did not look back, so you would not turn into a pillar of salt, but you left the corner house on Simón Bolívar where your parents, my adored grandparents, lived. I have never written about the Bolívar house, as you called it, Mama, because it is too painful for me. It is as if I were bleeding, being torn apart, because I still dream of that house every night. Someone closes all the vents and the doors are bottomless coffins.

Do you remember, Mama? The house on Bolívar Street was one of those inward-looking houses, it was like an interior gaze, like the most beautiful secrets. Everything was so luminous in the house on Bolívar, Mama, because there were birds and chicks, and you liked to hang the sacred leaves of autumn on the white walls, asking us to press our cheeks against them in order to greet the earth.

At times, Mama, you surrendered beside us in front of the wild vine that gave no shade but gave grapes, secret and juicy. Suddenly María walked by in her violet-colored clothes brought from the south, and she sat on the dewy grass that moistened her face and legs, enveiling her in the loveliest happiness, as if everything belonged to her, as if the dark and the light were jubilant mirrors steeped in the intensity of her delirious legs.

That was life, Mama, at the house on Bolívar. We were fascinated by time as it passed or did not, in love with peace. Everything seemed essential: our unhurried movements, elegant in their reticence, like postures of surrender. And suddenly we were no longer at the Bolívar house. Little by little the country turned into a fold of absence. It vanished before our eyes. It no longer is. Nothing is any longer. "Chile," you tell me, "I no longer know where to keep it, in my lost gaze or in my broken heart." But Chile was not what we lost, Mama. We were obsessed with remembering, because memory was hard and long, a gust of elusive murmurs. Your memory, Mama, was inescapable and digressive, and next to you we practiced remembering, because for you it was like breathing, like opening your arms and letting a garden of feathers shower our bodies.

Mama, how I loved you when at the beach your naked arms held us in the Pacific Ocean. I loved to smell you, Mama, and although lost, I recognize your scent. We climbed about your soul, your heart, like sea wolves. We loved you, Mama, and at your side the earth was delicious, life was tender and safe. Suddenly we packed our bags. You said we would hold Chile's first-ever garage sale, and all our dear possessions, little by little, became the property of strangers who nickled-and-dimed the price of each item. They did not care that the dolls had been brought over from Vienna by our grand-parents, or that my schoolbag was broken and empty. We packed up the house, Mama, and this time your arms became increasingly somber, their freckles exhausted. Your gaze became distant like the fog-covered hills. Little by little we lost things, time, the ability to feel, and we left, while the grandparents signaled us with gestures of love. Our isolation intensified. We got to America, the country of ab-sence, where no one is from anywhere, where we were merely poor Latin American Jews. No one loved us or paid us much attention. That's how we arrived, as if lost, in North America, sputtering words in English, clinging to Spanish. We were fragile and felt like gypsies.

Mama, you turned memory into a channel of return. What mem-ory? you ask. The memory of the Chile we left behind or the Eu-rope your parents had fled. Where did you place our memory? What could we make of it? Down which paths could we follow it? Who were we while we remembered? That is how we began to weave a life, guided by the passion of recollection at a senseless time in which memory was the end-all. We were constantly ambushed by endless questions. Where are you from? You always told them, as you gen-tly stroked your copper-colored hair and murmured in the direc-tion of the distant fog, "We are from South America." Innocent and malevolent, they insisted that we were too blond, too pretty, to be Indians. I'm sure you remember how they said you were much pret-tier than any Jew they had ever met.

Mama, we were always foreign, the outsiders, the refugees, but you showed us to love our difference, to be grateful for it. You told us, "Feel music, time, breezes and tangos with passion." Life with you was as light as your hair. You were lovely, Mama, and you al-ways smelled of the delights of gardens, of the chrysanthemums you rubbed into your skin. You were so alone when you came to America, as I am now, except that I have you to turn to when my children's teachers chide me for kissing my son and daughter too often. But Mama, you were alone. You left your entire history, your streets, and those times the ambulance came for you, full of dark, hooded figures, you were alone while death made conversation at the foot of the stretcher. You had lost your fifth child, yet unborn, and they took you off in the winged, reddish garb of fleeting love. You had left behind the balcony of your grandmother Helena's house, my beloved great-grandmother who cut out tiny paper figures and spoke German, saying that very soon they would come for her, out of her mind, emitting sighs of smoke. You left all this, Mama, and you brought us to America where I too live as a lost stranger, devoid of cities to invoke. I desperately cling to your story, to the memories you brought here wrapped in down-filled comforters.

I want you to know, Mama, how much I liked brushing your hair away from your forehead. I liked to feel your nearness, as you were every night, laying out our uniforms, kissing my forehead as only a mother can. I am alone, Mama, with my two beloved children, with a man I love who cannot know my history nor my origins of smoke. But as long as you live, my memory clings to yours, and I return to Chile to water our dead and think about how brave you were, Mama. I admire the courage it took to be an immigrant in America, explaining your background day and night. Jewish yet Hispanic, with an accent yet white, you were different from the Jews here in North America, to whom you had to explain that Latin American Jews existed, to whom you told your story only to overhear them say, "They are poor Jews."

You were wise, Mama. You say that nothing belongs to us, but on this lonely Passover I tell you that perhaps we do own words and love. I tell my children we should celebrate free nations and, as I write to you, I realize I have attained freedom, knowing that only memory and its uncertain metaphors are truly mine, belong to me. Here I am, Mama, like a woman in flight, writing this letter to you, because I want to say goodbye at last to the ghosts that surround the orchard of my dreams, and tell you that I have finished writing this story as I turn the age you were when you arrived in America. I have finished my book today, Mama, and now I can begin to tell you . . .

## My House

Silent and restless I approach my house that is my time and my story. We are in America. My mother lives at times grateful, at others in anguish. Yes, I know that I have lived in North America longer than I lived in Chile, and yet, I try in vain to populate my usurped childhood. I fill it with women, guardians of memory and temperamental ghosts. Since there are so few people left alive in my country, the cemetery is like a city I inhabit, and I visit my dead.

Memory plays and unravels the fragile threads of recollection. I ask myself, who am I? In which language do I recognize myself? How do I speak to my children: in Spanish or in English, or in both? But they answer: I am a foreign mother. They correct my English despite the fact that I speak it better than some who were born here. They correct the words I mispronounce with my strong accent, not artifice, but part of my language and my history.

Once again I ask, which is my story? Is it that of my great-grandmother Helena, gone mad as she looked at the enormous palm tree in Santiago de Chile, running terrified through train stations to commune with her dead sisters? Or is my story a childhood of holy cards depicting men tied to crosses in churches throughout a nation?

I live here, in New England, in a house like those of the previous century, shingled in white cedar. My town was never a whaling center, but I imagine it could have been one, where restless women pace awaiting the return of captains from the greenish sea. For me no one returns any longer. No one arrives. No one waves to me as they enter their homes. This is a close-mouthed, absent country, turned off. It is true no one returns any longer, not even I, because it is not possible to return. Where to go? Where is the city where I could resettle and tell one more story?

Here I am. The spring drizzle falls. The March winds do not calm my restlessness on earth. My children kiss me as they leave for school on an immense bus as yellow as a sunflower. Is this my story, at their side, next to their forever foreign mother?

# Chapter Seven

# Words: A Basket of Love

## A Basket of Books

In literature I found the caress, the unguarded pleasure, and the voice that had eluded me in this new country. I turned to books with a passion, almost in desperation, because they consoled me. I saw myself criss-crossing the hallways of the library, ransacking in particular the Spanish section and shelves. I discovered the warmth of words, words that belonged to me alone. I paused along their hills, invented the destinies of those exiled like myself. Above all I loved dictionaries, faithful guardians of my language. Through books I crossed borders. Wasn't Latin America an immense shawl united by a free and beautiful language?

My love of literature went beyond books as instruments of knowledge. When no one spoke to me or smiled at me, when I was told that in America one didn't do such things as drop in uninvited or eat eggplant, I went to the room of discoveries with my basket of books, like Carmencha with her bread. I read Neruda, Vallejo, Bombal, Cervantes. I read and I realized that this was life, the culmination of privileged moments, unrestrained happiness on my knees in the library. People passed by me like ghosts in the night, and perhaps that's what they were. This was America. I was hidden in the tropics, on glaciers, and the words danced in my ears.

## Books

Leaning against the books we played at spelling their textures. Before we knew how to read, books were paths, premonitory routes to happiness, invention found between the words. Everywhere books were alive. According to my grandmother, some of the books in our house in Santiago had been saved from the treacherous bonfires of Berlin. It was still possible to feel in them the presence of terror, the savage, sad skies between certain notched pages, pierced by fear. At times I would spread myself out on all the books that my grandmother left behind, Rilke's and Goethe's poetry, the family Bibles, and the books my father and grandfather burned in the bonfires of 1973 in Chile, books about the brain, Freud, and anything written by a Jew. Now I think about the shattered poets of Sarajevo, tearing the pages from beautiful books in order to warm their souls during winter nights. Books have been my traveling companions because I am from nowhere, and they provide me with the transfiguration of memory. Books help me to invent countries that I have visited in the forests of my dreams, to have certain faceless friends who, in the storm of exile, I took for my own.

In books, words are landscapes, prairies, steep mountain paths, and forests where a girl dressed in red inquired about her dead mother. So many books written to rescue and invent memory, so many books like slices of pain among the shadows, so many useless attempts at storytelling. One day, when I was still very young, I discovered geography books. There were books that seemed forbidden, dangerous books with drawings of the human body. Other books were birthday gifts, still books bearing witness to events beyond time and words. Impulsively, it occurred to me that I should leave the books propped up on the immediacy of the night table. Then I caress them, wish them good night, and imagine them dreaming in those cities where someone wrote a story for them. Books sleep in children's dreams. I dream the dream of stories not yet told and my lips begin to tell them out loud.

## Silences

The silence. The austerity of my dead words could no longer be my language. The silence. I learned English like a person feeling her way, on the sly and in the shadows of rented rooms. I reviewed the words, repeated them out loud: sun, light, peace. At times I hid in the closet with my pet, a flying squirrel, and cried.

The English language never took on the texture of my soul, the feel of my skin. It showed me the precision of detail, the melody of never-before-heard consonants, and I still must pause before uttering "th." After a long while I was able to love this language, because it belongs to my children, and I am amazed to see them love me and I them in that language. I speak to them in English about black angels and iguanas. I was never bilingual or bicultural. I let each language have its own soul, changeable and warm, free to embark on the dizzy tongues of mad poets.

I could not be in English what I am in Spanish, and yet I never tried. I never sought similarities between words or cities. I lived and live in North America as if by chance, as if my time here were borrowed, and at any moment I might strike out for a country where people speak not my exact language, but one close to it. To go to that land where nothing would surprise me, not the names of the streets or rivers. Then at last I would cease to exist in two languages, in two classrooms, split in half and belonging to no one.

## Languages

What does it mean to live in two languages, to exist on the border, not knowing when to cross from the realm of the mother tongue to the realm of the acquired language? Living through two languages is a marvelous thing, say the guardians of order, not memory. I only lived in one because the other did not adjust to my feelings or my skin. One language insisted on forgetting, the other on memory. The privilege of being bilingual and bicultural has its dangerous side. My mother's language I identified with love. English meant codes of silence. Spanish was silence and words. With it we invented parties that no one attended. We imagined the night wind blowing through the empty, frozen house. We found ourselves without a history, with no similarities to those around us. Mirrors returned the moisture of our faces, the austere solitude of our lives as strangers.

My mother taught me to speak the little English I still know. The two of us began with Shakespeare's tragedies and Milton's *Paradise*

*Lost.* I repeated out loud after her. Sometimes the silence, that which wasn't said, my inability to recite names of friends, made me believe I would never master English. So I lived with homework in other languages, autumn games, and a constant homesickness like a tingling in the body. I lost familiar objects and sounds in order to learn English, and realized that I existed outside of time. For me, life between two cultures was no life at all.

## Spanish

How I love my language. It is like the sky, high rooftops, and elongated words. Always in transit, all I was able to carry with me were my words. I took care of them, placed them in the moist womb of my pillow. I communed with them. Sometimes they made noises, like a garden, a threshold, lace and nighttime fragrances. I like my language. Looking up words in dictionaries made me happy and I found myself in words, because I, too, wandered lost along the avenues. I did not recognize myself, and no one recognized me.

Who was I in any other language?

Who called my name in Spanish?

Why did they make fun of my accent?

Why could the mere act of speaking out displace my tongue and brand me an outsider?

By contrast, my language loved me, sheltered me from the gray wind of deformed cities, of locked doors. I lost my keys and wandered among the omens of return. My language defined my past, it was relaxed and brave. The words, such ample, respectable ladies, were fraught with the possibility of love beyond diminutives. I never stopped writing in Spanish because I could not abandon my essence, the fragile, divine core of my being. It would have meant becoming someone else, frequenting sadness, losing a soul and all the butterflies. I always spoke Spanish, even in my most solemn dreams. I did not want to translate myself. I was Hispanic to the core and when, on the first day of school, I heard them tell one another not to speak to the Latina, I took a sip of water and wrote a line of poetry in Spanish. The line was so ancient, the words so deep, that I survived.

## My Accent

How could someone not want to lose this accent, want to cling to it as to life itself? I loved my accent. As far as I was concerned, it embellished the sound of English, softened words, warmed my lips with each emitted sigh, preserved the things I loved: angels, everyday words, sleepy mornings when I greeted my people in my language. Of all my belongings I was able to keep my accent, and to know that despite its strangeness, I am myself and my voice, looking toward the sun.

## Why Do I Write?

Writing is bewitching, like a song or cadence. I arrive at words the way one arrives at spells. Poetry is a story that attaches itself to my feet, my being. Sometimes I will lie down on the earth, invent poems about lost love and fear. Writing is a form of love, of loving and being loved. These aren't words, syllables, or useless alphabets launched by chance or an obsession with speech. Each word wants its own freedom to transform reality into wonder, to create another story, to uncover longings, happiness, the astonishing world between the pen and the shattered paper, limber and fragile. Writing is a way to truth, to telling the truth and tieing it to books, to stone walls.

As a child I wrote songs, poems, legends. When I was eight, I dictated my first novel to a friend twice my age, Elly Goldschmied. Every summer afternoon on Isla Negra, she faithfully transcribed *The Adventures of Rita*, and from then on, I could not stop writing. To have done so would have meant not to love, to exist, to breathe. I wanted to write about things invisible, nightfall in every desert, intrepid night and the silence of the syllables on the sand. I wanted to be faithful to the language that germinates and blooms like grass above the bodies we love. Then I captured in writing a taste of the country, the voices of women who speak as they fasten their skirts and carry fruit on their swaying heads like words.

Writing was a way to save others and myself. We were transparent in our invisibility. I wanted to know about each one of them, how and who they loved, what they did, where they lived. My words were like signs that led me to inhospitable, but always the most beautiful, regions. Then I encountered the memory of the dead in the Atacama Desert, and he told me: Yes, madam, I am also Jewish, and I know about prisoners. And he showed me the dwarfed bush growing on the Atacama Desert, where men had so often become inhuman, and had carved their history into dead trees.

To write meant to always be awake, willing to take risks, full of magic and happiness, eager to create and undo, because life was that way, like words. I wanted to be a word, that is, to be whole, making my life one with words, and so I speeded up my writing between dreams. I could not stop writing. I rushed toward the realm of words because they were like the blood pulsing uncontrollably through my hands. Writing was my bride, my vocation, my liberation, and above all, my story.

Then, when I left my language behind, and felt that loss like a mutilated body, I wrote about what was missing. I wanted to capture the pain of those who had been evicted from their lives. I wanted to tell about those who close their eyes. I wanted to speak of those places of honor where nothing blooms, yet suddenly the word, the disquieting voice of human life, surprised me and became audible. My work sprung from places occupied by outsiders, strangers, and absences. I revisited the past with obsession. My alphabet was made up of poems in search of a country. My passion was not nostalgia, nor the prudence of days gone by. My passion was writing because it allowed me to commemorate the faces of the disappeared. I did not want to disappear. Blindfolded, I could always find my way to the place of words, to the music of being or not being, to the zones of love within the circle of knowledge where time, seasons, and alliances coincide. Words gave me back my imagination. Words were fireflies, threads of transgression, of faith. Writing was not a hopeless return to the realm of enchantment or the silence of magic and mist that uncovers the light, but above all else the most intense pleasure, the brightest of all lights. Writing saved my life.

My writing and I were allies, companions, words formed concentric rings around me to combat the silence of what was the other. I wrote in order to feel the warm surface of my skin, to recall a lost voice, so that someone might tell me they loved me, or to invent another truth. Who was I in this human groundswell of diverse and secret, as well as open, hatreds? Was I so unlike the refugees from every war, those women on the street, proud and fierce about their belongings in small cardboard boxes?

Then I understood, and the revelation became my dwelling place on the golden thread that liberates me from all labyrinths: I am a Jewish writer who writes in Spanish and lives in America.

## The Leper Colony

One afternoon, after the ceremony of homework, after the green ink and the sky blue notebooks were put away, my mother told me that a letter had arrived for me. Her tone of voice was serious, halfway between perplexed and sweet. The letter was from a notorious and legendary place, Easter Island, where Chile maintained a leper colony, founded in the nineteenth century, far across the tormented Pacific Ocean. My letter was from there, and had been written by a leper who was looking for a pen pal. I still have no idea how he chose me. In those days lepers appeared in horror films, confined like lunatics or forbidding birds. Real lepers were incarcerated on an island almost as far away as Tahiti.

As I read the missive I felt pleasure and chills. How had this letter come into my hands? How did the writer know my name? What did this man look like, consumed by leprosy, destined to the lonely existence of the outcast, bound to the most terrifying silence and isolation? Naively I imagined that he had read one of my poems, but how did letters and poems reach his island? For that matter, how did a country as poor as mine manage cases of leprosy, the health care for these victims, frightening and hidden in a corner of the South Sea?

For many years I maintained a correspondence with the man or woman from this leper colony. I did not know his or her name, but I wrote from my earthly paradise to that of Easter Island. I did not want to sound awkward. I wanted my words to resemble the softness of murmurs. I told him or her about my adolescence and my full blown fears. At times I rubbed my letter against my cheek. I imbued it with an endless number of hidden signs, kissed it slowly, and imagined it imprisoned in a city pounded by the sea. I wanted to tell him or her about the passions of an adolescent imagining the sort of life, or the lack thereof, that a leper might experience far away on Easter Island, where nights were veiled in the shadows of sadness.

For a long time I heard nothing from my pen pal. The leper colony on Easter Island had shrunk, and one day its closing was announced on the radio. In this season of dead leaves I remember the lepers, lost in the immensity of the ocean.

## *Poetry*

On tiptoe poetry enters and leaves the orchards of dreams, galloping like a delirious toddler. That is how this visceral love of words came to me, words like the deepest nighttime spell, words like the chirping of crickets and predictions of good luck. In my short lifetime, words have been my companions, melodious friends offering tender, authentic love.

As a child I had the marvelous habit of talking to myself on the patio, in the secret corners of the attic. "There's the crazy-old-lady girl reciting demented words," they said. But I was not talking to myself. I was creating poems for the cats, the pine trees, the surface of each gust of wind, and the brooms, that were to me air-born flames.

To protect myself from spirits at night, I learned to recite out loud. In this way I banished the cavities of nightmares and invented new names for things. I spoke of women picking through trash and imagined them to be the owners of lost palaces.

Back then poetry resounded in my ears like an irresistible fragrance rushing through my body, demanding total devotion, like an angel accomplice. It had to be read out loud at night in the immensity of the infinite desert, the world beginning to grow in me. When we left for North America, I took nothing more than a book of Pablo Neruda's poems, because with him I could now say: "Tonight I can write the saddest lines." I was alone, no one spoke my language, no one knew my poetry, no one sat next to me because it was said that foreigners smelled bad. Poetry saved me from the depth of solitude, it gave me back my face and voice, filled me with water and stars and the golden braids of beguiled princesses.

Poetry was beautiful, young, and dressed like a river. I loved her, and with the gesture of a complicit bride, we joined one another. We went off, schemed words, and made love under a sky dotted with syllables, along an unhurried path.

## Words

Words like the fires of insomnia, like the stuff that fills memory. Words like the light of my memory. I collect them, I tuck them in beside me, I caress them and, naked, I press against their sounds alone. Then words begin to germinate within me, to water what has been left behind, and they take on names: hunger, spring, the width of my waist, the width of rivers. That is how I came to love them, like charms of peace. I kept them in coffers, in refrigerators, in the lining of my clothing, in my belly button. My words and I soared out loud, I elevated them to a song, a light. Cold and warm words were all I could take, along with the candlesticks and the feathers of my dead chicken.

## To Know the Night

He offered me a story. He told it as if it were a litany. At times his voice was loud and sonorous, at others, it was meek and quiet like the mushrooms growing in my country's forests. He took my hand that summer afternoon in a café full of ocean breezes and a feeling of happiness. This is how he began:

One night they called me because I was on duty in the village, an inhospitable spot deep in the desert of southern Chile where nothing grows. A woman agonized, I suspected from solitude. I asked what she wished to do in these final moments or days of life, and she told me: "I want to know the night." So I told her to go to Italy, where wine flows savagely during lovemaking. I told her to make love on tabletops, on the Amalfi shelves. I told her to live at the shore and dance with abandon. I told her all this, and she said, "Doctor, will I be capable of obeying you?" I closed the door to that room, that house, that life in the shadows, and I, too, returned to my rounds wishing to know the night.

Years passed and I heard nothing from her. I remembered neither her gaze nor her spongy body. Yet I still sensed what she had said to me: I want to meet the night.

One winter's evening of endless and deep mud, someone called me. A woman was in agony. I went immediately, and recognized the frayed roses on the large iron door. I heard the breathing of a familiar, even beloved person. She recognized me, took my hand protectively and told me: "I now know the night, and am free to die."

## Anne

Books illuminate the dark spots in the house. Books are like forests, strange dwellings, always secret. My father said that we were the people of the book and that even in dreams we completed the great book of God. On those occasions when I went to temple, I liked to kiss the Torah scroll, walk with it, embrace it because in that way I, too, could calm my fears of certain stories found in open books. Books that my father read at night, as if by reading them one could understand the silence that rules the house whenever they were opened; as if one could describe how many hairs from dead women's scalps might be needed to fill a room.

My neighbors read illustrated books, and books about angels. Everything in them had to do with faith, hope, and eternal life. I could not find rest in those books. That came only once I had read the diary of Anne Frank.

For many nights Anne Frank watched over my dreams, and I over hers, because we had been, perhaps, the same type of unruly, headstrong girl who loses the possibility of a more sacred essence, distances herself from what is remotely recognizable. Anne Frank was confrontation in a more daring, more innocent way, with wisdom and pain, as if in captivity, like a tenuous chrysalis. That was Anne Frank.

Little by little our bodies claimed space on a trip through luminous adolescence, toward fierce old age, in darkness. Anne Frank was lost, cut, and bleeding. She was like a friend who had vanished beyond memory, farther than the sea and its whims. And yet, she was a faithful nocturnal ghost, my implacable shadow, faith, and darkness. She was there with her thoughts, her madness that had nothing to do with perversity or anger. It was her, and more than that, it was the possibility of innocence usurped.

All through my adolescence Anne Frank occupied and watched over the ritual of my dreams. Often I woke up bathed in sweat next to my benevolent fears, and yet I knew her slightly. They allowed her neither to be a writer, nor wife, nor mother, nor a decent or indecent woman. Nothing of her remains, only her words, the most glorious form of memory.

Anne Frank is each of us, and beyond what each of us is and will be. Her diary does not contain photographs of trains pulling into the last smoke-filled station. She dared to speak of springtime's light, and the body of a girl becoming a woman. I like Anne Frank because she was no more nor less than ourselves, a schoolgirl. She spoke of awakening to excitement, of the rain in Europe. Even so, there was something more in Anne, beyond that first innocence, as if she were submerged in transparencies.

## Gabriela

She wore long, dark brown garments like those of the Carmelite nuns, and enormous men's shoes. That's what my mother told me about Gabriela Mistral, to whom she had the honor of handing a bouquet of violets when the poet visited her school in Osorno, near the southern meadows.

That's the way she was, Gabriela Mistral, the poet from Elquí. They said she was a strange woman who wrote crazy poems to lovers she never had, children. Brokenhearted, she wrote about mothers, the wide, lonely night, her solitude as a poor teacher.

I loved her poems. I recited them out loud in the morning light on the school patios, and alone at night when I told myself once more how much I loved lost things, and things that would never be recovered.

In the years I have lived away from Chile, Gabriela Mistral made me more American than all the Americans. She wrote about the smoke produced by the dark innocence of children and by poverty.

It was not the lexicon of political correctness but a burning flame in a bleeding heart.

Why did they want to erase my Gabriela with furious gossip? Gabriela of the valleys, daughter of democracy, light of the lost, today from this darkness of those without a country, I, too, call your name, a beacon in search of a country.

## Maria Luisa

My aunts lived in the sultry city of Viña del Mar. On certain holiday weekends, patriotic ones in particular, when the married women of the town wore yellow garlands and painted their doors blue, we did not go to Viña del Mar to visit the relatives. I remember that city inhabited by the thinness of fine, misty rain, the fog a fragile tulle on the hills, like a languid woman waiting for things to clear, for the first rays of dawn. There were enormous, dignified houses with disturbingly fragile balconies, where the servants rested on down comforters and listened to sensual soap operas on the radio.

Viña del Mar was not exactly the city of our childhood, but rather the city of our outings, small opulences, relatives who half a century later were utterly ruined financially. Above all, Viña del Mar was for me the city of María Luisa Bombal. "City that, were I blindfold, I would still recognize," said María Luisa Bombal as, distracted and without caution, she caressed the bark of certain abandoned trees.

María Luisa Bombal was the writer that Chilean schoolgirls most adored. We loved to approach her prose that contained the gesture of undulating words, and it was possible to still feel their warmth, the deepest caress of bodies intertwined after making love. To read María Luisa Bombal was for us, the uninitiated, a way of no longer being strangers to love, to ambiguity and wonder.

We liked her short books, brimming with intense journeys deeply rooted in the ephemeral and in happiness.

When my family went into exile in the seventies, María Luisa Bombal and her literature gave me sustenance, pleasure, the possibility of repairing a tenderness that had cracked. Years later, I traveled to Chile where I knew that we women writers were kept in the deepest, most hidden places of our idiosyncracies, submerged in the most lugubrious oblivion, in the most perverse disillusion of not being read.

My first memories of María Luisa Bombal must be placed in Viña del Mar, on a drizzly day. I, too, felt distant, trying to recognize the names of streets. Somehow I had returned to my country and promised myself that I would never be a foreigner. Suddenly I came across her house on the street with a beautiful name: Poniente 77. The house seemed submerged in frost, in the warmth of the luminosity of interior rooms where noise and silence play on rings of love. I knocked on the door, and there she was, noble and erect, dressed in black, her hair cut boyishly short. Around her neck was an oversized crucifix, much too large for a woman her height and with so many doubts about God.

We liked one another right away. I think that somehow we are twin souls, detailed about language expressing through poetry the clarity and tenacity of those who love writing. We spent many years in endless dialogue. María Luisa Bombal helped me to understand that writing was more than a job or vocation. She told me about her dark nights, her sleepless deliriums, and how many times all her characters arrived at the foot of her bed, including María Griselda, Ana María, the anonymous woman in *Ultima niebla*, she who does not wish to live another night without love, she who is frightened by the sight of her own hair, a flash of crowns deserted by birds.

I loved María Luisa Bombal for many years. I read her, laid bare what existed beyond the words, and steeped myself in her city, wandering through it, dreaming about it, trying to understand it. I found out that, alone and blindfolded, women who write are those who reach cities shrouded in mist.

## Sonia Helena

I
You are wise
to ask
the spirits,

your guardian angels,
to always be at your side
in light and in shadow.
It is enough to call them
by name
and you walk next to yourself
beside your forest gaze
to your river hands,
Sonia Helena,
my beloved,
let me draw close to the
edge of your dreams.

II

Sonia Helena,
abysmal interrogator
of the color of dreams,
you ask me about
ghosts,
whether they sleep in green clothing
in the thick of the forest,
whether they visit
mischievous children,
you ask me if
fairies change clothes
according to the way the wind blows.
I answer yes to everything,
I answer no to everything.
Ghosts watch
over the mischief of dreams,
fairies always
change clothes
because they are so diaphanous
and transparent and dress as if they were invisible.
Sonia Helena, I like that you are
dazzled by the magic
in your own small and valiant hands.

## Isla Negra

The sweet nighttime hours are like a thick forest. After so many years of clinging to the same dream, words spoken in strange languages fold and unfold, confused like hollow sunflowers at night. You ask me to tell you about my time on the islands, to whisper in your ear about the beat of your heart next to mine, like the most hidden, sleepy forest.

I will tell you about Isla Negra, about those summers when the days marched by, openly, perpetually, like the movements of water and light. I was wearing white because I was fifteen years old and my mother decided it was advisable to play with transparency. Then I went down to the beach where at times I saw Pablo Neruda, sitting motionless for hours, persevering half asleep by the great ocean.

His voice was also like that of the ocean, fraught with shadows and clarity. I knelt and slid my hands along the sand, sensing the moss of the steep rocks, the immensity of time hollowed above the starfish. I immersed myself in profound joy because that was life, and happiness was there, resting a moment in a watery garden.

The island meant contemplation of time outside of time, a mute heart gazing upon the bliss of nature unfolding. It was a world without a compass, a world attached to the storm of things, and I sensed the glory of being alive.

I tell you all this here, on the other side of America, where you do not know this tale, a talisman of memories, a precious crown. But this, too, is your story. It will live here, on this night of dreams, upon backs that turn like wheels. You tell me a story, and I will tell you one. It thrills me to tell you that I, too, love you, far from the islands, on the closeness of your skin.

## Pablo Neruda

I would see him, walking majestically. Sometimes he seemed to disappear from the world, then return to look at it once more. I liked to watch him, to pause over the most trivial detail of his beauty: small snails, beyond sound and human time, seaweed like the hair of luxuriant women. His gait and sense of wonder were slow, and no matter the season he wore an enormous Araucan poncho. At dawn, when the beach like a solitary woman recovers its spectacular beauty, he sat on the craggy rock, rolled up his shirtsleeves, hoping to capture the ocean's breath and stars, unfettered and free. He began to write, pressing against his knees, as if affirming his existence between the sky and the sea. His hands dreamed dizzily of cities inhabited by poetry. He seemed alone, yet full of love. That is how I saw him when I was a child. I saw and heard the women of the village say, "There goes Don Pablo." They did not call him Poet Neruda.

I liked to see him with his notebooks, pages dense with green ink, like moss and the peace of victory. I wanted to be a poet, too, and I learned to love things that unhinged and resembled absence.

For a long time, I saw Pablo Neruda walk along the coast of Isla Negra, and his presence inspired me to write.

## Goodbye, Pablo Neruda

In September the autumn breezes throbbed, and that great silence of sprites, fairies, and bitter dust could be felt up and down the avenues. Back then the streets and houses were empty. It was a time outside of time. The dictators cleaned the shiny streets with the faces of the embalmed dead. Then, on September 23, rumors spread of the poet's burial. Everyone knew who he was. He was nameless because his name belonged to all, as did his poems and words flowing from him like the fluid movement of the seasons.

Suddenly a slow cortège passed by, like the march of death, like the sighs of memory. They arrived with the sun, with wounded butterflies. Those empty avenues began to fill with the murmur of footsteps and breathing, a small seedbed of memories. All the laundresses came out with their white handkerchiefs, the young girls with their star-drawing pencils, the sad men, the widows, and the orphans.

Poetry was overwhelmed by the footsteps making their way through the throng of mourners. Their tongues gave more than life. Alongside the cortège, poetry also spoke. The poet's language became many languages. His widow looked skyward. She raised her arms, not pleading, but in victory. From the stilled voice in the casket came many voices of lovers who had hidden beyond the avenues, of secret, clandestine love affairs.

In my country, when they buried the poet, the land became a carpet of flowers. Among the tears were smiles, and for an instant, the night of the dictator gave way to the day's victory. A man had died, but not his words. Pablo Neruda had died in his house by the sea.

## The Stone House

When we left our country during the military dictatorship, I lost my own face for years. There were no grottos in Georgia, and my head sank into my pillow, into the red earth. Soldiers surrounded Neruda's stone house, but the faithful, with their passion for life, inscribed its gate with poems and placed small, enchanted wildflowers in front of it. The house became like a sleepwalker. It was alone, but the words lodging in it are immutable. Years later, when the tyrants in heavy, thrashing boots fell from power, the house was opened. We returned to Chile with courage and dignity, and were able to go inside. Like mischievous children we played with the model trains that light up the surrounding landscape. Respectfully, we picked up the poet's secret belongings and put them away, our joy flowing through the windows toward the Pacific Ocean. The bells, fraught with the smell of ocean breezes, shaped like waterfalls and waves, were still there. They were the reason why I wanted to return, to keep the memory, to recover my mother's tiny stones, to pick blazing aromo flowers that are like robust tangles of sunlight.

Today I return to the Chilean coast with my grandmother, who is almost ninety, and my young son. I tell them to press their faces against the rocks that taste of secret grottos, that are as tall as the stars and the treetops, and they do as I ask. I lean against them. At last I have returned home. I trusted in words and poetry, and the country is once again decked out in its very best clothes.

# Chapter Eight

## Returns

I

Irascible from so many journeys,
forgetful in the
cities of the
aged,
the traveler seeks
the permanence
of leaves within
the childhood forest,
of greenish butterflies.
She returns to the garden
predicting the
birth of
geraniums.

II

She does not wish to know
monuments
nor rituals.
She wants

a house among the
bonfires.
She made
her altar of dreams
on which were placed
two or three
naked angels
and the names of
dead women.

## Memorial of Oblivion

One day I returned to my country. There were no generals or men
of death lying in wait on every corner. There were only moments of
mad happiness, like gusts of wind from the mouth of God or the
beaks of birds. I felt it on certain mornings while walking through
the city, saying hello to everyone I met. It seemed as if these were
my people, and my words entered a dimension in which time is sacred and the rituals of Paradise are performed. That was happiness,
a gust of wind, like a wave of crackling fragrance tumbling from the
gazes of people who were not strangers.

## Homecoming

Like a joy that draws near in the intimacy of memory, like a tickle
at once soft and distant, could that be what it feels like to return? The
fragile gaze at what we call our country? How is it possible to de-
fine one's country in this century ablaze with horrors? Why do I
love this place that forced us into exile, that punished my father for
being a Jew, that permitted the dismembered silence of the dead and
the complicity of the living?

Time and again I peer out the window of the airplane dancing
above the desert hills of the Atacama. We are flying over northern
Chile, and I recall the goodness of that mute, present desert, which,
with devastating silence and impunity, preserved in its salty womb
the violated bodies, the massacred bodies. Suddenly I feel memory

once again smacking its lips like a sleepy, moist foam. I recall the names of certain flowers, the wonder I had felt at night under the cloudless sky, sonorous and open. Then I vaguely understood that my country is that intensity of experience, a celebration of the alphabet, syllables cinching my waist. My country is a first kiss, a freely spoken word, a rumor of hope in the apprenticeship of feeling.

I am alive. Even blindfolded and forever orphaned I recognize this landscape. I have arrived in Chile. All my dead are here. This is the land that tenderly covers them and lends permanence to my uncertain pilgrimages. My feet touch the humid earth at dawn. I stumble against the pulsing trees and know that I am of this uncertain earth, between mirrors and water.

## The Street

Life was there, in the street, between cloudbursts and orange blossoms. It was a jumble of languages. Tongues wrapped themselves in the pleasure of words. I loved to walk down the street because life was there: on the palate, in the pleasure, near the blossoms. I liked to stroll slowly, to simply be, to feel the hand-clapping, to be a breeze between thick chunks of air and light. It was my air, my city, my rivers, and I named them like someone who hums a much loved song. It was my street, with flower vendors who asked, "Some violets, miss?" It was the street, with its music and history, the passion of its memory. I approached the gypsies and fortune-tellers with fake necklaces and real stars. I was happy, intrepid in the forests, and I knew myself to be complete and beautiful among people, on the street, in life. I knew I was a friend among strangers.

## To Be a Stranger

Then I recognized myself in the voices of others, voices that were like my own. Only at that moment, at the beginning of speech and all sayings, did I realize I was from that other place, that I belonged to them. Despite all the time that had passed, all the flights and the crotches of light, I am not asked where I am from. Everything returns my gaze, and only a few stairsteps were surprised to be accompanying me to your house, the house of love. Suddenly the afternoon wind settled on my tanned shoulders as it did when I was young, and desire was mute like a restless heart deep in the forest.

I recognized the butterflies and the omens of death. I recognized myself as I wrote poems of love and rejection. I recognized myself in the fragrance acquired by my voice and my skin as I returned, now a woman, to that summer of lives retained and distant. That was me, in a country I had left as a girl, under cover of night more than seventeen years before. Was I the same person who walked through the wheat fields, searching for myself among thick van Gogh brushstrokes?

And yet, I was the one measuring my own steps, touching the ground with happiness, with the certainty that I had never really left. Why did the men selling straw recognize me? Why did the wind create furrows like caresses of desire in my hair? This was what it meant to be from somewhere. It was something very simple, like reciting the same childhood poems, knowing which streets are best for kite flying, being able to trill the songs of birds that live somewhere in the sky. This was my return, even if only for a while, knowing that I would leave and once again suffer the constant interruptions of others who, once they heard me speak, would ask where I was from, that I would once again sever the roots that had remained behind in the south, at the far end of the earth, in a country called Chile, where poets were beloved and my eyes still awed by all beginnings.

## Escape

I remember that my nana buttoned my green coat, as she did on cold days as I prepared to leave for school. She tried in vain to smooth my angry, defiant hair. I didn't know what to say to her. She simply kissed my ear and sat me near the eucalyptus tree. I promised I would take care of myself, and return to her the way hands return to rituals of flour. The fog was very dark. In the distance sleeping animals predicted our return.

I no longer remember our flight, only our homecoming: the wind grazing our cheeks, the familiar night smells, and the distant ocean, always violent and pacific, always the ocean. She came to the door half naked, like a figure in a dream, and welcomed us. Yet each time we returned, there were fewer people to greet us, so many had died, so many had left, and I knew that I would share their fate.

To leave and return, but to return in the dark as if feeling my way, return through veils of memory. I caress the earth still there, and sense that she, my old nana, sleepwalks through the old house, dusting its musty, scratched furniture. She speaks very slowly about the return of the jasmines and the damn eucalyptus that overruns the garden. I still love her and hear her voice, still want to unbraid her jet hair. But she, the old Araucana, has lost her hair, the light, and the voices. She dusts the house of the dead, and someone has told her to light a candle at night to frighten away the souls.

I dreamed or invented such a homecoming, but in truth my return was not sweet. Rather, it was the nightmare of things gone away.

## With My Children

Then I imagine my return, hastily arranged, as if all I had to do was cross the street, walk into the deepest woods, and there I would be. But then my recollection changes at the far end of the treetops, beyond all transparency, and I know that none of my friends remain, that they all fled through the mountains, disguised as other things so as to be accepted as perpetual strangers. Nevertheless I stubbornly return, time and again, and each time more urgently. I repeat the names of the trees, and very late at night, the names of the stars, as I watch the Three Marys. Now I return with my children, and they hear me say that there is a long, narrow country almost at the end of the world where the deserts and the ocean blend in a wild sort of landscape. There, in my country, beloved people still experience happiness, leisure, good conversation, the language of poets, and the unhurried language of love. I tell them that and they, too, prepare to return, to become reconciled to the mist, the sparrows, and immutable time.

## *An Invitation to Travel*

He brought along nothing but his eyes. He had very few possessions, but I asked him to travel with me to the lands of Chile, and he, my son, drew close to my face and offered me his hand. I felt all the warmth of his skin, a garden of wild foliage. And: "Yes, Mommy, I will go with you to that torn and distant territory that you dream of at night, asleep and awake. I'll cross the immense heights of the landscape with you. I'll see the condors and the women so beautiful that they come out to collect the dead, and to wash fruit wilder than that of their faces among the shadows."

So he and I set out on this journey that was neither beginning nor end, neither return nor flight. I wanted to traverse my childhood through his gaze, wanted his gaze to invent my own, his hands to whiten my laughter. All sadness was cleansed by his smile.

## *My Childhood*

Summer with its long, illuminated nights, summer with its fragrance of roses and wine, the fire of fireflies in love. I draw close to the fragrance of this night, where the preciousness of time was a watery substance, where nights waft oregano and cilantro. Their fragrance is born of the earth, resembling a happy apron. I want to tell you about my childhood, Joseph, about that long, narrow country of deserts, of windstorms, at the edge of an ocean as blue as your eyes and dark as a vast well. On this summer night, long and extended like a hand that conjures up the places of memory, I want to tell you about the murmurs and the footsteps of my childhood in a country called Chile, amid the fragrance of bells and birds populating the sky like a chrysalis. Then, when they ask you about that country enveloped in smoke and windstorms, you will know what to tell them. Tell them, as the world nears its end, that happiness lies in the simple contemplation of roses, wheat fields, and crows in love. This country called Chile, where your mother studied her primer, among other journeys, and then one day moved away with her mother. Her grandmother gave them a handful of earth and a bit of flour and sun within which to cultivate nostalgia.

## Sonia Helena

Together we descend to the sound of leaves, a fleeting labyrinth of leaves. You are growing up during autumns that are like enchanted gardens. We have tumbled down this waterfall of leaves. Your dress blurs with yellow, your hair weaves the wind's ardent dance. You are growing up during autumns that guard fast the season of caution. Suddenly I feel we are at the ocean's edge. The leaves are sea salt, soaking us and erasing our names. The wind blows from the Andes, a southern wind foretelling good or bad harvests. We are not among the leaves, my daughter, I tell her. It is the ocean playing at our feet, the Pacific Ocean striking the palms of our hands, dazzling as flames. Playfully you shower me with seaweed. Then I realize that you will not know that sea, the bodies torn open on the rocks. You have not grown up in the south, but in autumnal New England. You will not speak the words of the south, nor will I be there to remind you of the salt on the cheek of the air, on the ocean's wise, untamed palate. You are growing up during autumns in gardens of shadows.

## I Tell Them We Are from Here

Suddenly, I descend at the end of a long journey like the subtle noise of dreams. I descend very slowly. I do and do not recognize the landscape, as if it were a matter of certain streets, of childhood memories that are no longer ours when we return. But this was, and perhaps will be, my country. The descent is very long, like memory and oblivion. I return time and again, and even if they were to blindfold me, I would feel the subtle warmth of the southern wind. No longer is anyone lurking in wait to terrorize us. No one is there, just the secret and still dead.

But before the descent I see the northern mountains, small and mysterious cavities like the sense of touch, desire, or passion. And those mountains that draw close to my country are everything I have loved and not loved. They are the police and the fairies, they are the dead and their guardian angels.

Gradually, I descend further. The flight attendant strolls with assurance through aisles of air. I hug my children next to me, and tell them that this is my mother's childhood, that here is where the blind hen played, that here blood brushed up against her legs and beyond. They, wise children, understand it but do not feel it. I do not understand why I left, why I lost my speech, my words, all my beloved letters and games on the corner, the bewitched hands of the women who combed my hair and rubbed lavender water all over my body.

Suddenly I arrive here, at the end of the earth, and my memory fuses with those of others, and they in turn become my memory. My tongue approximates the words I abandoned, and there is a sense of freedom, despite the fact that nothing belongs to me, nothing that I have loved has been and will continue to become lost. We have arrived, says an ungrateful voice, and only my ninety-year old grandmother awaits us. She has spent an hour on the balcony in a city on the sea waiting for her offspring, so few in number, to be at her side, in her arms, in her memory. We have arrived, they always say. I cannot speak. I arrive at this other edge of America, the end-of-the-earth America, spread open and mine. From a distance someone calls me. It is the wind, and I offer it a slice of our sweet, pure air. We have arrived, I tell them, and the day changes color. Time, borders, memory, and forgetting are no longer. This is where we are from, I tell them.

## The Pools

There were the pools. That's what we called those immense enchantments of water and cloudy sand. To get to them, one had to descend rocky streets, confused paths covered with giant foliage, and there were the pools, small watery ruts and smooth rocks, majestic in their ancestral simplicity, fresh islands of transparent water. There I rehearsed my first kisses, on my own moving body where the water lengthened my hair and my breasts acquired the quickness of mirrors. There were the rocks upon which my mother rested her copper-colored hair and dreamed. There were the immense chains of rocks assuming their destiny in fertile and in barren times.

I told my son: This is where I played with your grandmother. Here she taught me about the alphabet and waterfalls of songs that resembled prayers or the first secret murmurs. I also told him that sometimes when my hands scraped the night, I saw the first sighs of those who defy the secret silence of love. He, too, understood that the pools, once earth, were now a memory, a sigh, and he loved them because I did. On the quickness of all breaths, the two of us walked single file along all the steep rocky paths, and recognized fragrances, the immense transparency of the air, the sounds of peace and war. Because we thirsted for the sea, because we expected nothing but life itself in all its abundance, because the prudent and wise rocks were there, and the soul defied all vertigo and every abyss.

## Traveling the Length of My Country

I wanted to travel the length of my country, to extend myself across its territory, to be an archipelago or a ribbon of broken islands. More than anything, I dreamed of the north and its violet deserts, and the violent truth of that land of beheaded ghosts. I traveled to the north, motivated neither by pleasure nor a happy tourist's curiosity. I needed to apprentice myself to the secrets, to that which goes beyond time and silence. The desert offered the truth: the salty matter, the sun, the intrepid wind that had preserved the dead bodies. Now, with their mouths gagged and their eyes blindfolded by loops of rope and cloth, they rest in a large, dark pit where empty shoes and paper flowers cover their bodies.

I went to Chacabuco, Pisagua, and Calama. In each of these cities the living told of their dead, how they were found, how some are still being sought in the savage midday storm.

The north of Chile is like the heart of its people: intemperate and wild. Everything there seems frozen in time, full of fragile, forsaken flowers, cut open like a moaning mirror. But the sand, the dryness of the rocks, the mute landscape, seem to harbor truths and memories and they give them up wrapped in flour sacks found throughout the nation. How not to speak of them?

The north of Chile is a vast silence. The emaciated wind moans and slips by, traveling the length of the tombs protected by the sand. The hands of the wind knew how to gently cover those children of the desert. The desert knew how to care for them. They went to die in the desert because that was their destiny, because only the desert and the words of the wind would manage to tell the truth.

They were good, these countrymen of mine. They were your

brothers. Someone decided to blindfold them, and take their lives. Someone decided they should not see another dawn, and that's what happened. The desert men died with their bodies underground, with murmurs of empty longings. They lived there for many days, forgotten, and the entire country refused to see them. But the desert cared for them, preserved their memory and that of the living.

I return to the distant north, my forehead covered with saltpeter and the hardness of poor men. I also take with me the nation's open heart. All of Chile is a bleeding desert. Chile is the men found buried in the sand, and in the distance the accusing wind, the wind that tells all, and the sand a tender mother.

## Calama

They, the women, makers and seekers, asked me to go with them to the other edge of my country. This time I obeyed their call. I joined them as a lost traveler looking for other women's children, just as my cousins who, after the gas chambers, the faded, humid war, had searched for their family members and neighbors. Yet not a single voice spoke out to tell of what remained. Then as now, voices had withered and dried.

It is very hot and I am in northern Chile where every day is a fire without a past. These women, widows all, have asked me to travel with them to this far-off place, where the desert is an unbroken horizon. These women, these widows from Calama, have asked me to help search, because a voice told them that their executed, bullet-ridden children, hands tied behind their backs with small strips of silk, are there.

We go, and the trip leads us beyond the confines of hell. Suddenly I hear the voice of my great-grandmother, murdered at Auschwitz, and my aunt who died at Treblinka. I am here alongside these widowed desert women because I am a Jew, and they have asked me to come with them. The night seems to drift off course. The night is the heart of a dark well. Everything is so vast and dark in this nebula of widows in the desert. I walk with them and throw stones. We want to name the stones, but there is only oblivion, and open wounds blending with footprints in the sand.

At noon or at midnight we kneel. We cannot distinguish day and night. Only we recognize one another in this grave search, and I kneel alongside them. With the feathers of dead birds we bury ourselves in the sand, look for them amid the dunes, as if on the threshold of a dream before the wars. Suddenly we find a severed hand, and it draws us near, giving us hope. We say this hand is ours, and we love it with the clarity of visionaries. I, too, find the toes of a sleeping child. We are no longer alone in this ungrateful, sinuous, and vast desert.

## Desert Light

We had begun the journey as if hypnotized, erased by muteness and thirst. We did not know how long we were together on that crossing. Perhaps we were alone, like those couples who live inhabited by shadows of an always fleeting love. There was nothing in that landscape, only a merciless wind, the wind crackling through the gully-ridden earth, the wind like a tired violin. Even in the breeze my hair did not move, but my lips exclaimed. They were thirsty and did not know how to ask for water, or to say that here, perhaps, someone had loved, on these earthen mounds, in these sandy hollows visited by perverse and mischievous death.

Tears welled up in my eyes when we traveled through the Atacama or the Sinai because those beloved deserts were now unloved. They were full of dead people. All Chile, all Israel, fit in that dense dirt. I restrained my own hands. I wanted to die. My ears buzzed. I felt that my body was not my own. At times I saw myself, my body lying in the desert, and I was alone, totally alone in the solitary vastness.

Much of the air floated skyward. It was a strange air, like a supplication, because its noise resembled distant, numb voices, trembling and terrifying, from a time without hours, a time belonging to no one. Yet I was surrounded by mere sand and hills, a nameless, godless landscape.

Then we arrived. Something about the place provoked noise, people. Something about the place made me feel the dead were there, crouched in the very faces of the dry shrubs. But there were no shrubs. There were no birds. There was no one, nothing. Only the guardian of the dead, or of memory. He said to us: "Welcome, friends, to the concentration camp," and I thought of my aunts burned at Auschwitz. I saw their faces for the first time. They did not moan, but could not quench their own thirst. Those were my dead aunts, and I saw them that day.

The guardian of life and death showed us the cell. There were no marks, no footprints. Suddenly a lizard appeared between the walls and told us to go to the only tree in the camp. The tree was dry and bent like a man in agony, its limbs parched and twisted. He contained all their names: those who agonized, those who thirsted, and those who defamed love and shelter.

The dead were there, sleepless. They were cold, they were hot, no one could quench their thirst or their speech. What were the dead saying? There they were, receding into the shadows, fleeing. What would they have thought about this new life?

I wept so copiously that I saw a small shrub kneeling at my feet. I listened to the music of the wind, strange melodies of victory. Somehow it told me that the dead were dancing behind the breeze, like a school of fluttering fish. The sand, the salt, the flamingos in the desert river had sheltered them. They were there, and I wanted to dance with them, abide with them.

This is what I learned at the Chacabuco Concentration Camp on January 2, 1996. Everything I have told you is true. I felt more Jewish than ever in that camp. Someone yanked out my hair and shaved my head. We left the desert and its voices. My hands were unable to remain still. Knotted, they clung to yours, because among the shrubs of patio 26, facing the tree in agony, I had been savagely wounded. I wanted to be them, to leave, to remain forever in the air alongside the dead of Chacabuco. My children called to me. They were on the coast, near the sea during the season of green breezes. I returned from the dead, leaving a part of myself behind. I headed north, far from Chacabuco, where the desert is more than a desert. It is the wind that splits the skin, a moaning flute like the muzzled bodies of the dead.

## The Bonfires

At times my mother's and grandmothers' memories, transfigured and well-traveled, move to the beat of my own, and I become confused.

I don't know whether I recall or invent the stories they told me after dark. I remember my great-grandmother saying books had been burned, and in a distant forest, they had begun to burn women. I remember her terse, undiminished voice, and sometimes at night, when noises carve a wide, drowning hollow in my memory, I wake up either in Vienna or Berlin. I am in Santiago de Chile. Soldiers in enormous, evil jackboots, their hands imprisoned as well, are burning books, and over there, in nearby neighborhoods, I see familiar bonfires.

## The City of Strangers

Faced with the premature darkness of night, the city is a stranger navigating through shadowy zones. The night, the sudden blackness, locations and everyday faces made unfamiliar. I walk along, knowing that not a single nook or alleyway will lead to the grotto of my memory. In this city no one recognizes me. My childhood was never a part of these streets. Nothing conveys intimacy or plenitude. In this city I no longer know the names of the trees or how to get to a particular corner. Perhaps this is exile: to walk through a city where the past does not exit, where being a stranger is like a distant, other silence.

Faced with the night I approach the city. In vain will I try to traverse and memorize its streets.

## High Treason

Treason is a way of life, she said. It is brave because people wish it so. That's how it has always been. For fifteen years she slept in her clothes, not clandestinely, but in bright reds and pinks, and in luminous slippers. They never came for her.

We are at the Universidad Católica of Chile in Santiago, where they killed a professor right there, as he walked down the stairs after class. They killed him for being an informer, but more than anything else, for spreading his ideals, like poisoned juice. We are a nation of traitors. Treachery marks us. The auditorium doesn't seem worried by the quiet laughter. The young people, accustomed to hearing of the previous generation's horrors, don't say anything. There is only a vast silence, the immensity of silence. I hear it because I have come from abroad. I am self-exiled, and that is why they judge me. I am Jewish and that is why they judge me. I have dedicated myself, generously, to bringing literature written by others to the attention of the world, and that is why they judge me. This is my country. People speak of happiness in terms of their most recent acquisitions, as consumers. We are a nation of traitors. Women have been tortured near these classrooms. They have been forbidden to return to their studies. Other women, professors, are informants, too, but we don't speak to one another, we don't recognize one another. This is my country, a democracy of fragile words, like a necklace of birds. And from the gallery, laughter and more laughter. I tell them yes, we are a nation of traitors.

## *María*

### I

Then she plunged her hand into mine. I still perceive her fear as well as her warmth. Something in her confirmed the silent predictions. We were afraid of words because they had paused in the ruts of silence, but we spoke the way women do once the heart has split open, once we have lost the season of clarity.

She told me in a hoarse voice, like a child beginning a story: "This is a gift for you. Do with it what you will." We held hands. It was a drizzly, misty day. She said: "Yesterday I found this photograph of myself, taken before he took me away, and I still do not recognize myself. I have lost my ability to see, and all the dominions of life are foreign to me. I look at myself in this photograph. I was seventeen years old. Perhaps my mother sold me into prostitution so that I would have an easier time, and take full advantage of my Scottish last name. It invited wealthy men to sleep with me. I carry this photograph with me. It is lonely like a path at summer's end or a sad and sunken road."

### II

I heard her, I sensed her. My voice became thin. I stopped, too, and began to look at the photographs. They are more than ten years old, I tell her. Yes, she repeated, those ten years, so distant and so present. Two tall young men came for me. My mother said they were decent people, they were fair-skinned and well-spoken. They told me to go with them, and I went, covered from head to toe in a fog. I could not see nor name the stars. The darkness was timeless, noiseless. It was the malevolent, opaque darkness of horror. It was the darkness of the dead. They took me into the hills, along overgrown paths, and asked me to speak and not to speak. I only felt that we climbed and descended along vertiginous roads, and my heart opened. It didn't sigh, it opened.

### III

I descended. I went up. I thought of Dante in the infinite second hell. They stripped me naked. I descended. I went up. I went down. Their hands traversed my eyelids and my breasts. They asked me my name and when I told them, they did not believe me. One of them told me I was a politician from Viña del Mar, and they entered between my legs, they pierced my dignity. They usurped me. They broke me. They tore me apart. They spit at me. I knew nothing of escapes and returns. I only remembered that photograph that they took of me when I was seventeen, that photo which I cannot stop telling you about because perhaps it contains the rhythm of love.

I listened to her and trembled. Suddenly the ocean that protected us became a single staircase that rose and fell and moaned. A staircase that stole the sound and texture of time from us. I gazed at the photograph knowing that they had forcefully taken her sight, her eyes, her passion for life, life itself.

### IV

They sent me back, she said. They sent me back in pieces. I could no longer feel. I was skin and bones, and there were tiny spiders encrusted in my body, which sighed like a fan. My gaze was deep, like concave wooden boats. Nothing about me was memorable or recognizable because I was dead, empty.

When I got home, my mother didn't ask. She told me that the neighbors had not found out and that my boyfriend had called. I couldn't tell her what they had done to me. I couldn't tell her about the stairs, the savage screams, the women who scoffed at my nude body and urinated in the shadows, my inaudible moans.

I left the country, far from the gags, and I didn't speak for more than twenty years. The truth is that everything here has died. The country has become a purgatory of tormented souls.

V

As she spoke, my face contorted as if I, too, wished to find her. I imagined the stairs, the savage screams, as if someone or something were tearing her heart from her chest. She told me that her mouth lost its smell, the fragrance of the body lying in grass, the warm summer on the edge. I heard her for a long time. What was time? In what corners had the crannies of memory become lost? I thought of her returning home, and of her mother wrapped in complicity and fog.

VI

Suddenly I said to her: "The worst thing is that we are not a nation. We are wasted, solitary islands that conjure the savage rhythms of terror." I placed my hands on her forehead and kissed her. That was my gift, a kiss to a forehead marked by footprints and cracks. Her voice grew thin. She resembled things lost in the tides. She was like painful, disturbed sleep. Again she spoke to me about the photo. It was your adolescence, I told her, and she replied by shaking her head. I descended beyond dreams where packs of hounds nest, where eagles pause, where censors inhabit the realm of death.

I drew near to her face. I wanted to restore her ability to taste memory, so I gave her another photograph, one of myself.

## Cecilia

Back then, Cecilia, your words were like ingrown wounds. For years you maintained the clearest possible silence, as if your voice were a flame among the embers beyond the distant ashes. I began to remember your hunger one illuminated night in Valparaíso when the imaginary, imaginative poets arrived at your door of ashes. That night you prepared a magical, fragrant dinner, adorned with oregano, boldo, wildflowers, rice, tomato. I tell you, dear Cecilia, it was the most lavish dinner I ever experienced, and we shared it, together.

Now, Cecilia, democracy has supposedly returned to the south. General Contreras is in jail, and you have just begun to speak. Back then you were afraid to speak, but did so because loneliness is like a sorrow lost in the entrails of night.

Back then you spoke to me about hunger rather than the void, the absence, the savage humiliation, the pain that mourned in the breath from your mouth, in the hollow of your stomach, on the bronzed surface of your skin. Back then you told me about the butcher who assumed you had three dogs because you bought so many horse bones with which to make soup for your children. You told me all of this, my dear Cecilia, and your eyes broke my heart. Your hunger was shared by all of us who lived mutely, who did nothing in the face of the immense night.

## Violeta

You arrived, Violeta, with your eyes resting upon the night. You arrived unhurried because you waited for an ineffable, eternal time, that time when the shadow of death sniffed your pain-filled gaze. You always arrive, Violeta, because you wait for me, acknowledging those who love and do not forget you. How long we searched for you, Violeta, how many sleepless Andean nights, how many cold metal doors and gagged mouths.

Violeta, you have spent twenty years looking for your brother Newton and still you recognize yourself in diaphanous mirrors, unfrightened by your mute expression. I still cannot shield myself from the light of your eyes, the warmth exhaled from the clear abyss of your gaze.

It is springtime, Violeta, and I have returned to Chile. Or will I always be returning to join my memory to yours? Although I am alive, Violeta, something in me also died, broke into a thousand pieces, ceased to exist, to be, to recognize the earth. I inhabit the strangeness of languages that will never be mine. I survived, Violeta, in order to find you, to help you search for your brother, and console your mother who has lost her mind and continues to call his name.

I like to be with you, Violeta, to look into your eyes, still amazing and bright, like two ferocious, velvet grottos. I like to hug you, Violeta, and tell you that many are at your side. You are not alone, Violeta. On November 1st, Chile will be covered in flowers. The entire country will be a field of wildflowers, and on each petal we will find them, all the Victors, the Gonzalos, the Marías, the dead generations that still live as long as you seek them, Violeta, with your worn shoes and ghostly gaze.

## The Sound of Women

Then the city dawned amid the sound of old women who foresaw time and air as a gash. I have returned to my city, or perhaps I never left it. I traveled with my hidden self, positioned between the darkness and a sea of suffering. Wherever I went, that city went with me. But now I am not there, I no longer recognize myself in my own house, nor in the gardens where I once played and carved the word *love* in the trunks of trees. Everyone in my city has died, or lives as if dead. When I arrive I plan to go to the Jewish cemetery to leave stones on my grandfather's grave. I plan to go to the plaza where I used to play with Luchito before they blindfolded him now and forever. My city is like a corpse full of dead people and fragile phantoms begging to be heard, begging for a sliver of time in the storm, begging to see the sun.

The city is inhabited by specters of all that was. Solitary and lost men dissolve there, gray men with their gray overcoats early in the morning, coming from and going to strange jobs. My city wakes up silently and I barely hear her because the dead make no noise as they move about.

I have returned to her in an alternative, truncated search. I have found myself alone in a hotel room, watching scintillating treetops, remembering the flower-filled spring mornings when nothing seemed to bother us, a morning when we walked unhurriedly through the city. Suddenly the smoke arrived, the ashes, the bombs, the black sky with its words of war. An assassinated president foreshadowed streets filled with tortured bodies, but in the end, history would deem the victims men of justice. I have come to the city to go to Salvador Allende's grave to give him a carnation. I have come as one who wishes to visit the Andes, the spaces of war, because I am here and I am not, I am alone and with companions, I wonder who I was and who I am. Why did I have to abandon times and latitudes? Why do I write, inventing a language I barely heard, living in a kingdom of borrowed dreams and letters? Why did I have to leave my country, leave life, my childhood, adolescence, all suspended in time? My cousins, my birthdays, my bosom filled with dreams, all stayed behind in Chile. What color mourning clothes should I don in this far-off place?

I think about it all on this morning in September. The Chilean dictatorship does not seem like yesterday's faded memory, quite the contrary. It is alive and still among us. Like a faithful tattoo, fascism clings to skin and faces. Their heads bowed, Chileans walk as strangers unto themselves, accustomed to the law of silence, and the city seems like any other. Fascism does not need violence to thrive and it adheres tenaciously to the skin like fear. Fascism is the reconciliation to oblivion.

Then I knew that perhaps we had left in order to be free, in order to be welcome in, or at least not excluded from, other strange countries. This morning I woke up alone in a hotel room. I know none of this belongs to me and that the dictators had stolen my heart.

## A Divided Heaven

All through the night he undresses then dresses me, as if my clothing were petals to be peeled from my flesh. He says I am a lost, far-away rose. I love him because I am a child in love with the old poet. Because he is like that which died for me, and now, back again in my homeland, it all returns to me. I like his words, I listen to them until I can no longer hear because his caress upsets me.

I entered his mouth as in a dream. It was full of birds and words. At times the words were sticky, like the disturbing caress of an old man, a clever lowland wolf, perched between my legs, pausing before the secret imperfection of my desire. Is this what love is like? I asked myself in the dark, light-filled rooms. That was love made mad with the reddish heat of words I never heard before.

Desire played alongside an older man during the summers,

confusing winters of my adolescence. That night I slept with him. I wore a red dress. He told me I looked like a dead angel. That's how I began with that man on a distant beach, in that house facing the ocean, and with black birds perched on the thresholds.

## Desire

All night long I gather your frozen body before the islands. All night long I gather the crazed wind that puts the nude body in relief. In the distance, the women's boats float, empty. In the distance those boats waited for the men to return from the sea. I was cold, and you said you would kiss my ankles. I was afraid that someone might stab your pillow as it covered my dreams. You offered me a head full of white hair, and I dreamed of thread, spindles, and love.

I don't know how much or why I loved an older man who could have been my shipwrecked grandfather. After his death, I returned to my country as an orphan, and you were there, offering me a basket of words and the keys to the island house. You gave me your hand in which to shelter my sparse, frightened baggage.

That night my body molded to yours as if they had been old friends keeping one another company. I traversed your bent neck, and your face changed in the clarity of my hands. Having searched so hard for something permanent, I found you, who never left the beach house, and saw no one except disobedient girls like me. Our frenzied lovemaking taught me that desire was like a wild journey across two bodies.

## Summer's End in My Country

More than any season we loved summer, with its bells of silky wind, with those yellow dappled meadows and our young bodies drawn close to the flowers, the woods, and the water on our feet. Deliriously we moved along the thick grass. In those days the homeland was honorable. Our happiness stemmed from the knowledge that life was a single celebration. Years later the country was stained, ocher and yellow, summers meant draughts, and the wind became a thin, voiceless gust. No longer did people wish to acknowledge their neighbors. We greeted one another from afar, and in confined places unfortunate lizards nosed about. Summer took on the face of misfortune. The homes of poor and rich alike were boarded up. The country became speechless and we, too, went far, far away.

## New Year's Day 1997

In the distance, someone launches the first flame of the New Year. The hills are dotted with small fires and barefoot children come down from the highlands, holding small stars in their hands. The night slips off course and the port of Valparaíso burns with love. There are no longer rich and poor. The streets resemble an immense carnival of gestures and human arms, and in the simple words, "Happy New Year," I gleefully find myself. A few minutes before midnight I hug my dead grandparents, my cousins who perished wearing somber parachutes deep in the mountains, my uncle seduced by alcohol. I greet my dead, those buried here in Chile, whom I visit every year. I return because this is my country. I come back to the land itself, the flame of memory, and I say, "Happy New Year, Chile." The word Chile is moist on the tip of my tongue, and with that tongue I pronounce the names of those who have gone and those who are present. My country is barely audible. I am the girl who asks about lost things, and I am the woman who manages to find herself among the embers. My memory is like air, fleeting and bold.

With only a few minutes left before midnight, I go out on my grandmother's balcony alone. The O'Higgins Hotel is completely illuminated, its nineteenth-century façade an incongrous presence amid the more authentically Chilean buildings. In that hotel full of somber and seigniorial rooms, the highest officials of the Chilean navy met to plan the military coup of 1973. Back then the cities of Viña del Mar and Valparaíso were full of marines speaking in foreign voices and languages. North American, South African, some Israelis made up the fatuous force of armed volunteers, the secret seducers of power. In that hotel my grandmother and other elderly residents of the building waited together for the earth to calm during the ominous earthquakes throughout the history of my country, my luminous country of catastrophes.

The air tonight, also luminous, is moved to pity, because it is my very own air, so recognizable and palpable. It fills the night and wets my lips. It is the air that saw me grow up. And now, again, I watch the small fires in the houses of Valparaíso like small bats in the immense heart of this summer night. I touch myself, smell myself as I did before, feel my skin singed by the passing sun. Nothing and everything has changed, because I am the one who left.

## A Place of Memories

Hidden and so secret, like nighttime scabs, my grandmother had stayed behind, reassuring her memory with permanence. Perhaps that was the meaning of aging, to let go of false belongings and to dedicate yourself to collecting moments as if it were a breeze passing above the clouds or a garden of leaves in the spirited crackle of winter.

My grandmother, with her golden furrows, had stayed in Chile, and thus assured my returns to that place that was no longer my country. At that time Chile was a place of memories. I could recognize certain street corners or reminisce about the gauzy, transparent blue dress that I wore to my first teenage party, where I hid in a bathroom.

When I returned to Chile, the country had donned clothes fit for precarious mourning. Conversations evaporated like mist, like the closed-off corners of our souls. The dictatorship had made us a country of strangers, of men and women in hiding, slipping fearfully along the avenues. When I returned my grandmother was present, eternal, ceremonious. For me, Chile does not exist without her. She was sure, like the permanence of stones. She took us home and during my stay I heard the same old stories that this time around seemed less my own. Even the language was now at arm's length, and beloved words sounded as if they were spoken by others, people I had never known nor met.

Suddenly, I went out onto the nighttime balcony, my grandmother's balcony. I had often gone there to linger in the orchard, in the slow, sure blooming of the lavender. This was the balcony that had taught me to look, and to raise my hands and body above the cadenced shrubs that ring the cement. I saw the hills through the fog. Exile was being in a fog and trying to decipher familiar signs and sites. Light fell on the hills, and I turned to see women dressed as brides and widows descending toward me. Only then did I know that I had returned, that remembering was the permanence of certain images in motion, subtle images rooted in the land of dreams.

My grandmother draws near, perplexed. She gives me an accusatory look, as she often did when I was a child, but her accusation and anger are affectionate because her authority is kind. She scolds me because I did not put a shawl over my shoulders, because I have been outside too long, and I go back indoors with her, hugging her frail shoulders that seem smaller and smaller to me, as if a young, frightened angel would at any moment carry her off.

I return to the room where a hot-water bottle awaits me. I pull up the covers as in fiercest winter. This is my place. I recognize myself not in objects, but in the certainty that I have been in the floorboards and bookshelves, that I have lit this night light as a person wrapped in love. I recover it all. That afternoon, in the stone house by the sea, I reoccupy old spaces.

My grandmother is ninety years old and she admits not wanting to age. That's how she delays the eyelids of death. She is innocent, my Josefina, but we call her Chepi, an old habit of linking her name to tenderness. I repeat the same things, light the same lamps, return to the same rooms, and in that familiarity of permanence, try to recall a nation that has changed. Here in Viña del Mar, at almost forty-two years of age, I begin to reconstruct my memory, knowing that it is not really my own. I recall a childhood that did not take place here, imagining how things might have been, reinventing myself through memory.

## Night

Night falls along the coast. The lights and hills continue their blinking ceremony. I have trouble falling asleep, but strain to recognize the rivers and the passage of flowers at night like a poem that opens and closes. Sleep overtakes my body. This is a city surrounded by mist, and although it is not my city, it is my place. In the distance, in the room next to mine, my grandmother repeats dreams and messages. She has made me return, and I draw close to her face like a wild stone, precarious and intense, the stone of memory, of pain and happiness.

## Old Age

Then I would go from room to room to make sure that the things I loved and did not love were still there, polishing the surroundings with my gaze, photographs of all the dead relatives, bits and pieces of things, the doves accustomed to the happiness and filth that caress my past. Her walk was slow, yet it embraced every bit of space, like those neglected plants that grow at night. Then I knew that this was old age, the rhythm of things in repose, the meditated good-byes. That's what my grandmother was like at the age of ninety, her breasts and legs on night's final watch, like the stories of smoke and her own ghost from all the houses. She walked in circles, her eyes reddened, and death was the guardian of all that is infinite.

## Rice Powder

She begins to let go of the beads she used to lend to us children when we were sick or stayed home to rest. She no longer wants or expects anything. Days become confused with nights, and her memory withdraws to the beginning when the beauty of her own face brought happiness to her equally beautiful soul. My grandmother still likes to look at herself in the mirror and touch up her face with one of those old-fashioned, lovely powders she collects and that her grandchildren and friends bring as gifts from abroad. She applies it to her face and creates a somber, translucent chiaroscuro, a face that quivers between light and shadow. She begins to talk to me about her house, her garden, days by the sea, and her face shines. In her old-woman eyes I see summer and green things. Suddenly, on the other side, the dark side of her face pocked by age, which shows no mercy on skin, I see small gullies and secret cavities, and she tells me: "It is Death who sleeps on the thresholds of my eyebrows."

I still like to surprise her in the bathroom facing the magic mirror and doing her face, dark on one side, light on the other.

## The Roommate

Then I would hold her face between my hands like a great moon, waning but still luminous. I would wipe the rice powder from her skin and say to her, "Grandmother, you are still afraid of Death, your roommate." She would grasp my hands, meld them into her own, and say, "Is it very noticeable, my darling girl, this chill of death that coats my skin?" And I say, "Don't be afraid of the kind roommate who has been at your side since the day you were born." My grandmother smiles, and I run my hand over her face so I won't forget it.

As much as we await it, and during certain misty moments wish for it, death is always untimely. Death and its ambivalence, like something hateful, like being underground, no longer aware of the rain, of faith. My grandmother with her rice powder and my humid hands on her face of air.

## Death

The mirror no longer reflects her gaze, and so she invents other unsettling, luminous images of self. Death deliberately trips her, makes fun of her, yet they take pity on one another, aware of that one wild certainty, that irreversible goodbye to consciousness. My grandmother insists on living, on recovering the light of her extraordinary eyes resting on letters that become ever smaller and more distant. Language no longer belongs to her and her memory teeters. "I'm getting old," she tells me. "I cannot distinguish light from shadow. I am aggravated by sordid chores of days without books, and yet I don't want to die. Life is being here, being present, speaking and not speaking." Then I kiss her and allow my body to blend into hers. I take her by the hand, as she once did to me, and we go into the garden so she can sense the light of the lemon trees and the warmth of the jasmines. "I want to live," she tells me, and I draw close to her, invent secrets to tell her, unspoken whispers, and we return to a previous time when, newborn and full of wonder, she could not distinguish light from shadow.

## The Last Goodbye

So you have given up your struggle with death, Grandmother? I ask myself whether you might even welcome it a bit. You always feared it, and that's why you never looked at covered mirrors and were terrified by the Jewish rite of wrapping the dead in a white sheet. How many times did you tell me that you trembled at the thought of death's footsteps, the sound of her golden shoes in the gravity of night. But now, perhaps you wish for her. You tell me you are going blind, that the universe is a collection of cloudy figures; that you can no longer read the daily paper nor discuss the destiny of the British royal family. The owner of the corner newsstand used to save you copies of any magazine featuring the royals because they were the most expensive and glossy. But now you cannot even read those. All the letters have been torn from you and life seems merciless.

As I draw close to your face I am greeted not by death but by all the gravity and weight of old age, the twists of memory and the heavy load of forgetfulness. Where are you, Grandmother? What sacred forest lights your way? I have been so close to your life, and you to mine, helping me to invent it, I tremble at the passage of this solitary, cruel time in which all senses become mute, and life moves in frightened slow motion. You no longer hear, Grandmother, yet you can still imagine the Viennese waltzes and a few poems you used to recite for me. Now it is my turn to return them out loud to you.

At night I kiss you, not knowing what to hope for you, whether to wish that an angel accompany you to your final resting place or ask for one last confidence. Malicious gossips and good friends alike have said you were adopted. They say that your mother, wild and sweet Sonia, conceived you with a lover, far from Odessa. At the hour of your death, all questions are pointless, all gestures useless.

All that is left is to hug you, Grandmother, run my hand through your still golden hair, repeat once again the motions of love, tell you not to fear death, that it has been at your side, a faithful neighbor, a sweet companion.

I take my leave from you, Grandmother, and our goodbye is ever more inevitable. I know that I will lose my name, your memory, that I will no longer return to you, nor this country, nor this house by the sea because I, too, will go with you, Grandmother. There will be no one with whom I can share my fears nor my journeys. But that, too, is inevitable, and all that remains to be said in this last goodbye is that I love you and will love you in all things on which love rests.

## Copihue in Bloom

Unexpectedly, my restless, blurred dream appears, like the color of still honey, sunflower yellow, sleepy and luminous. I close my eyes to acclimate myself to the provinces of all my memories. In the distance, the hills, the brilliance of the trees with names and the uncertain transformed by words. I recognize myself in front of the house, the orchard, the wild grapevines. I am a small girl, mischievous and mute. My mother is hanging fresh laundry near the lemon tree, and she herself seems to be made of light.

The landscape takes on the shape of my body, small and winged, folding and unfolding. At times it lengthens, and I recognize the scent of life, the obedient roses that flower each year. Here in the south of the world, life is diaphanous. Days transpire unaltered until death arrives, also diaphanous and peaceful. Suddenly I hear a voice that calls, insistently, and says: "We must gather our belongings." My mother packs the suitcases, her hair uncombed, and my father knows he can take neither the piano nor the microscope. They begin to call and we sink into a detestable rush. Now I am no longer mute. I silently cross the texture of other languages. They want me to constantly translate myself into someone else, and I want the tenderness of recognition and the privilege of my own happiness, at home, in the south of the world. I wake up and know there is no going back. At my side my husband dreams other dreams, but my legs intertwine with his. In his sleeping, distant body I will perhaps find my house, the flowering tree, the grapevine, and the copihue in bloom.

## Guest

As an attired guest
I returned to my country,
a frightened foreigner,
I first recognized
dry rivers
the darkened mountain range
assiduous traveler of the dawn
I later found fitting refuge
in the shadows.

My dead
stirred.
The youngest did not know me,
my language,
my face,
furrowed by other suns.
I was the absent relative,
the expatriate aunt,
the eccentric obsessed with justice.

Nor did I recognize
myself among strangers.
Every step in each city
an extended farewell
without love without ire,
simply the perplexing and light
absence of what does not remain
further removed like absences
like love affairs in strange cities
or travelers exhausted by leisure.

I was a guest in my country
in vain did I try to resemble
those who had stayed
and yet,
my speech was a sharp blade,
I was unable to name flowers,
nocturnal cacti.
I lost my country
and gained a continent
and why not the Earth.
In my empty hands
I held colorful maps.
My gaze recognized
neither blocks nor buildings,
only the windstorm that loves and whistles
and a ghostly woman
flying above the cityscape.

# About the Author

Marjorie Agosín is an award-winning poet, short story writer, and human rights activist. She has received numerous awards for her work in human rights, among them the Good Neighbor Award, the Jeanette Rankin Award for Human Rights, and a United Nations Leadership Award for Human Rights. She is also a recipient of the *Letras de Oro* prize for poetry and has written two memoirs about the life of her parents in Chile, *A Cross and a Star* and *Always from Somewhere Else*. Her most recent books of poetry are *Dear Anne Frank*, *An Absence of Shadows*, and *Desert Rain*.

Marjorie Agosín is professor and chair of the Spanish department at Wellesley College. She lives in the town of Wellesley, Massachusetts, with her husband and two children.

# About the Translator

Nancy Abraham Hall was raised in Mexico, D. F., and is a senior lecturer of Spanish at Wellesley College. She is the translator and coeditor (with Marjorie Agosín) of *A Necklace of Words: Short Fiction by Mexican Women*. She is also coeditor of *Campo abierto: Lecturas sociopolíticas de Hispanoamérica*. Her translations of poetry and fiction have appeared in numerous anthologies.